WITHDRAWN

STACKS

THE NINTH AMENDMENT

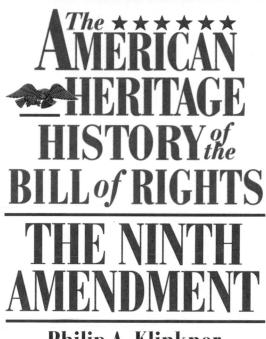

The
AMERICAN
HERITAGE
HISTORY *of the*
BILL *of* RIGHTS

THE NINTH
AMENDMENT

Philip A. Klinkner

Introduction by
WARREN E. BURGER
Chief Justice of the United States
1969–1986

Silver Burdett Press

To Marie and her generation. May they protect and expand the rights and liberties of all Americans.

Cover: Some people claim that among the unenumerated rights protected by the Ninth Amendment are the right of students to acquire knowledge, the right of teachers to teach, and the right of people of all economic groups to equal education. In 1973 the Supreme Court ruled that absolute equality of education was not guaranteed.

CONSULTANTS:

Maria Cedeño
Social Studies Coordinator, Region 4
Law-Related Education Coordinator
Dade County Public Schools
Miami, Florida

Michael H. Reggio
Law-Related Education Coordinator
Oklahoma Bar Association
Oklahoma City, Oklahoma

Text and Cover Design: Circa 86, Inc.

Copyright © 1991 by Gallin House Press, Inc.
Introduction copyright © 1991 by Silver Burdett Press, Inc.

Published by Silver Burdett Press, Inc., a division of Simon & Schuster,
Inc., Englewood Cliffs, N.J. 07632.

Library of Congress Cataloging-in-Publication Data

Klinkner, Philip A.
   The Ninth Amendment/by Philip A. Klinkner: with an introduction
by Warren E. Burger.
   p. cm.—(The American Heritage history of the Bill of
Rights)
   Includes indexes.
   Includes bibliographical references.
   Summary: Discusses the origins and provisions of the Ninth Amendment, which protects
"unenumerated" rights, or rights not listed in the Constitution.
   1. United States—Constitutional law—Amendments—9th—History
—Juvenile literature. 2. Civil rights—United States—History—
Juvenile literature. 3. United States—Constitutional law—
Interpretation and construction—History—Juvenile literature.
{1. United States—Constitutional law—Amendments—9th—History. 2. Civil rights—History.} I.
Title. II. Series.
KF4558 9th. K55 1991
342. 73'085—dc20
{347.30285}
                                                                    90-20068
                                                                         CIP
                                                                          AC

Manufactured in the United States of America.

ISBN 0-382-24188-6 {lib. bdg.}
10 9 8 7 6 5 4 3 2 1

ISBN 0-382-24200-9 {pbk.}
10 9 8 7 6 5 4 3 2 1

ONTENTS

$\mathscr{I}$N T R O D U C T I O N

WARREN E. BURGER
Chief Justice of the United States, 1969–1986

The Constitution does not specifically list all rights of the people. The Ninth Amendment was added to the Bill of Rights to reassure the people of the late 1700s that "we the people" retain certain rights even if these rights are not listed in the Constitution. Many students of the Constitution think that this was one of the amendments that was not necessary. In essence, the Ninth Amendment emphasizes that the federal government has only those powers given to it by the Constitution.

Concepts of liberty—the values liberty protects—inspired the Framers of our Constitution and the Bill of Rights to some of their most impassioned eloquence. "Liberty, the greatest of earthly possessions—give us that precious jewel, and you may take everything else," declaimed Patrick Henry. Those toilers in the "vineyard of liberty" sensed the historic nature of their mission, and their foresight accounts for the survival of the Bill of Rights.

Despite its significance for the theory of our government, few if any cases have ever been decided on Ninth Amendment grounds, although minorities on the Supreme Court have suggested that they are prepared to do so. Thus no rights have been identified as rights protected by the Ninth Amendment, and so far no court has found a power claimed by the federal government that is "reserved to the States . . . or to the people."

The long-term success of the system of ordered liberty set up by our Constitution was by no means foreordained. The bicentennial of the Bill of Rights provides an opportunity to reflect on the significance of the freedoms we enjoy and to commit ourselves to exercise the civic responsibilities required to sustain our constitutional system. The Constitution, including its first ten amendments, the Bill of Rights, has survived two centuries because of its unprecedented philosophical premise: that it derives its power from the people. It is not a grant from the government to the people. In 1787 the masters—the people—were saying to their government—their servant—that certain rights are inherent, natural rights and that they belong to the people, who had those rights before any governments existed. The function of government, they said, was to protect these rights.

The Bill of Rights also owes its continued vitality to the fact that it was drafted by experienced, practical politicians. It was a product of the Framers' essential mistrust of the frailties of human nature. This led them to develop the idea of the separation of powers and to make the Bill of Rights part of the permanent Constitution.

Moreover, the document was designed to be flexible, and the role of providing that flexibility through interpretation has fallen to the judiciary. Indeed, the first commander in chief, George Washington, gave the Supreme Court its moral marching orders two centuries ago when he said, "the administration of justice is the firmest pillar of government." The principle of judicial review as a check on government has perhaps nowhere been more significant than in the protection of individual liberties. It has been my privilege, along with my colleagues on the Court, to ensure the continued vitality of our Bill of Rights. As John Marshall asked, long before he became chief justice, "To what quarter will you look for a protection from an infringement on the Constitution, if you will not give the power to the judiciary?"

But the preservation of the Bill of Rights is not the sole responsibility of the judiciary. Rather, judges, legislatures, and presidents are partners with every American; liberty is the responsibility of every public officer and every citizen. In this spirit all Americans should become acquainted with the principles and history of this most remarkable document. Its bicentennial should not be simply a celebration but the beginning of an ongoing process. Americans must—by their conduct—guarantee that it continues to protect the sacred rights of our uniquely multicultural population. We must not fail to exercise our rights to vote, to participate in government and community activities, and to implement the principles of liberty, tolerance, opportunity, and justice for all.

THE AMERICAN HERITAGE
HISTORY OF THE BILL OF RIGHTS

The Bill of Rights

AMENDMENT 1*
Article Congress shall make no law respecting an establishment of religion, or prohibiting the free exercise thereof; or abridging the freedom of speech, or of the press; or the right of the people peaceably to assemble, and to petition the Government for a redress of grievances.

AMENDMENT 2
Article A well regulated Militia, being necessary to the security of a free State, the right of the people to keep and bear Arms, shall not be infringed.

AMENDMENT 3
Article No Soldier shall, in time of peace be quartered in any house, without the consent of the Owner, nor in time of war, but in a manner to be prescribed by law.

AMENDMENT 4
Article The right of the people to be secure in their persons, houses, papers, and effects, against unreasonable searches and seizures, shall not be violated, and no Warrants shall issue, but upon probable cause, supported by Oath or affirmation, and particularly describing the place to be searched, and the persons or things to be seized.

AMENDMENT 5
Article No person shall be held to answer for a capital, or otherwise infamous crime, unless on a presentment or indictment of a Grand Jury, except in cases arising in the land or naval forces, or in the Militia, when in actual service in time of War or public danger; nor shall any person be subject for the same offence to be twice put in jeopardy of life or limb; nor shall be compelled in any criminal case to be a witness against himself, nor be deprived of life, liberty, or property, without due process of law; nor shall private property be taken for public use without just compensation.

AMENDMENT 6
Article In all criminal prosecutions, the accused shall enjoy the right to a speedy and public trial, by an impartial jury of the State and district wherein the crime shall have been committed, which district shall have been previously ascertained by law, and to be informed of the nature and cause of the accusation; to be confronted with the witnesses against him; to have compulsory process for obtaining Witnesses in his favor, and to have the assistance of counsel for his defence.

AMENDMENT 7
Article In Suits at common law, where the value in controversy shall exceed twenty dollars, the right of trial by jury shall be preserved, and no fact tried by a jury, shall be otherwise reexamined in any Court of the United States, than according to the rules of the common law.

AMENDMENT 8
Article Excessive bail shall not be required, nor excessive fines imposed, nor cruel and unusual punishments inflicted.

AMENDMENT 9
Article The enumeration in the Constitution, of certain rights, shall not be construed to deny or disparage others retained by the people.

AMENDMENT 10
Article The powers not delegated to the United States by the Constitution, nor prohibited by it to the States, are reserved to the States respectively, or to the people.

*Note that each of the first ten amendments to the original Constitution is called an "Article." None of these amendments had actual numbers at the time of their ratification.

TIME CHART

THE HISTORY OF THE
BILL OF RIGHTS

1770s–1790s

1774 Quartering Act
1775 Revolutionary War begins
1776 Declaration of Independence is signed.
1783 Revolutionary War ends.
1787 Constitutional Convention writes the U.S. Constitution.
1788 U.S. Constitution is ratified by most states.
1789 Congress proposes the Bill of Rights
1791 The Bill of Rights is ratified by the states.
1792 Militia Act

1800s–1820s

1803 *Marbury* v. *Madison*. Supreme Court declares that it has the power of judicial review and exercises it. This is the first case in which the Court holds a law of Congress unconstitutional.
1807 Trial of Aaron Burr. Ruling that juries may have knowledge of a case so long as they have not yet formed an opinion.
1813 Kentucky becomes the first state to outlaw concealed weapons.
1824 *Gibbons* v. *Ogden*. Supreme Court defines Congress's power to regulate commerce, including trade between states and within states if that commerce affects other states.

1830s–1870s

1833 *Barron* v. *Baltimore.* Supreme Court rules that Bill of Rights applies only to actions of the federal government, not to the states and local governments.

1851 *Cooley* v. *Board of Wardens of the Port of Philadelphia.* Supreme Court rules that states can apply their own rules to some foreign and interstate commerce if their rules are of a local nature—unless or until Congress makes rules for particular situations.

1857 *Dred Scott* v. *Sandford.* Supreme Court denies that African Americans are citizens even if they happen to live in a "free state."

1862 Militia Act

1865 Thirteenth Amendment is ratified. Slavery is not allowed in the United States.

1868 Fourteenth Amendment is ratified. All people born or naturalized in the United States are citizens. Their privileges and immunities are protected, as are their life, liberty, and property according to due process. They have equal protection of the laws.

1873 *Slaughterhouse* cases. Supreme Court rules that the Fourteenth Amendment does not limit state power to make laws dealing with economic matters. Court mentions the unenumerated right to political participation.

1876 *United States* v. *Cruikshank.* Supreme Court rules that the right to bear arms for a lawful purpose is not an absolute right granted by the Constitution. States can limit this right and make their own gun-control laws.

1880s–1920s

1884 *Hurtado* v. *California.* Supreme Court rules that the right to a grand jury indictment doesn't apply to the states.

1896 *Plessy* v. *Ferguson.* Supreme Court upholds a state law based on "separate but equal" facilities for different races.

1903 Militia Act creates National Guard.

1905 *Lochner* v. *New York.* Supreme Court strikes down a state law regulating maximum work hours.

1914 *Weeks* v. *United States.* Supreme Court establishes that illegally obtained evidence, obtained by unreasonable search and seizure, cannot be used in federal trials.

1918 *Hammer* v. *Dagenhart.* Supreme Court declares unconstitutional a federal law prohibiting the shipment between states of goods made by young children.

1923 *Meyer* v. *Nebraska.* Supreme Court rules that a law banning teaching of foreign languages or teaching in languages other than English is unconstitutional. Court says that certain areas of people's private lives are protected from government interference.

1925 *Carroll* v. *United States.* Supreme Court allows searches of automobiles without a search warrant under some circumstances.

1925 *Gitlow* v. *New York.* Supreme Court rules that freedom of speech and freedom of the press are protected from state actions by the Fourteenth Amendment.

1930s

1931 *Near* v. *Minnesota*. Supreme Court rules that liberty of the press and of speech are safeguarded from state action.

1931 *Stromberg* v. *California*. Supreme Court extends concept of freedom of speech to symbolic actions such as displaying a flag.

1932 *Powell* v. *Alabama* (*First Scottsboro* case). Supreme Court rules that poor defendants have a right to an appointed lawyer when tried for crimes that may result in the death penalty.

1934 National Firearms Act becomes the first federal law to restrict the keeping and bearing of arms.

1935 *Norris* v. *Alabama* (*Second Scottsboro* case). Supreme Court reverses the conviction of an African American because of the long continued excluding of African Americans from jury service in the trial area.

1937 *Palko* v. *Connecticut*. Supreme Court refuses to require states to protect people under the double jeopardy clause of the Bill of Rights. But the case leads to future application of individual rights in the Bill of Rights to the states on a case-by-case basis.

1937 *DeJonge* v. *Oregon*. Supreme Court rules that freedom of assembly and petition are protected against state laws.

1939 *United States* v. *Miller*. Supreme Court rules that National Firearms Act of 1934 does not violate Second Amendment.

1940s–1950s

1940 *Cantwell* v. *Connecticut*. Supreme Court rules that free exercise of religion is protected against state laws.

1943 *Barnette* v. *West Virginia State Board of Education*. Supreme Court rules that flag salute laws are unconstitutional.

1946 *Theil* v. *Pacific Railroad*. Juries must be a cross section of the community, excluding no group based on religion, race, sex, or economic status.

1947 *Everson* v. *Board of Education*. Supreme Court rules that government attempts to impose religious practices, the establishment of religion, is forbidden to the states.

1948 *In re Oliver*. Supreme Court rules that defendants have a right to public trial in nonfederal trials.

1949 *Wolf* v. *California*. Supreme Court rules that freedom from unreasonable searches and seizures also applies to states.

1954 *Brown* v. *Board of Education of Topeka*. Supreme Court holds that segregation on the basis of race (in public education) denies equal protection of the laws.

1958 *NAACP* v. *Alabama*. Supreme Court rules that the privacy of membership lists in an organization is part of the right to freedom of assembly and association.

1961 *Mapp* v. *Ohio.* Supreme Court rules that illegally obtained evidence must not be allowed in state criminal trials.

1962 *Engel* v. *Vitale.* Supreme Court strikes down state-sponsored school prayer, saying it is no business of government to compose official prayers as part of a religious program carried on by the government.

1963 *Gideon* v. *Wainwright.* Supreme Court rules that the right of people accused of serious crimes to be represented by an appointed counsel applies to state criminal trials.

1964 Civil Rights Act is passed.

1964 *Malloy* v. *Hogan.* Supreme Court rules that the right to protection against forced self-incrimination applies to state trials.

1965 *Griswold* v. *Connecticut.* Supreme Court rules that there is a right to privacy in marriage and declares unconstitutional a state law banning the use of or the giving of information about birth control.

1965 *Pointer* v. *Texas.* Supreme Court rules that the right to confront witnesses against an accused person applies to state trials.

1966 *Parker* v. *Gladden.* Supreme Court ruling is interpreted to mean that the right to an impartial jury is applied to the states.

1966 *Miranda* v. *Arizona.* Supreme Court extends the protection against forced self-incrimination. Police have to inform people in custody of their rights before questioning them.

1967 *Katz* v. *United States.* Supreme Court rules that people's right to be free of unreasonable searches includes protection against electronic surveillance.

1967 *Washington* v. *Texas.* Supreme Court rules that accused people have the right to have witnesses in their favor brought into court.

1967 *In re Gault.* Supreme Court rules that juvenile proceedings that might lead to the young person's being sent to a state institution must follow due process and fair treatment. These include the rights against forced self-incrimination, to counsel, to confront witnesses.

1967 *Klopfer* v. *North Carolina.* Supreme Court rules that the right to a speedy trial applies to state trials.

1968 *Duncan* v. *Louisiana.* Supreme Court rules that the right to a jury trial in criminal cases applies to state trials.

1969 *Benton* v. *Maryland.* Supreme Court rules that the protection against double jeopardy applies to the states.

1969 *Brandenburg* v. *Ohio.* Supreme Court rules that speech calling for the use of force or crime can only be prohibited if it is directed to bringing about immediate lawless action and is likely to bring about such action.

1970 *Williams* v. *Florida.* Juries in cases that do not lead to the possibility of the death penalty may consist of six jurors rather than twelve.

1971 *Pentagon Papers* case. Freedom of the press is protected by forbidding prior restraint.

1971 *Duke Power Co.* v. *Carolina Environmental Study Group, Inc.* Supreme Court upholds state law limiting liability of federally licensed power companies in the event of a nuclear accident.

1972 *Furman* v. *Georgia.* Supreme Court rules that the death penalty (as it was then decided upon) is cruel and unusual punishment and therefore unconstitutional.

1972 *Argersinger* v. *Hamlin.* Supreme Court rules that right to counsel applies to all criminal cases that might involve a jail term.

1973 *Roe* v. *Wade.* Supreme Court declares that the right to privacy protects a woman's right to end pregnancy by abortion under specified circumstances.

1976 *Gregg* v. *Georgia.* Supreme Court rules that the death penalty is to be allowed if it is decided upon in a consistent and reasonable way, if the sentencing follows strict guidelines, and if the penalty is not required for certain crimes.

1976 *National League of Cities* v. *Usery.* Supreme Court holds that the Tenth Amendment prevents Congress from making federal minimum wage and overtime rules apply to state and city workers.

1981 *Quilici* v. *Village of Morton Grove.* U.S. district court upholds a local ban on sale and possession of handguns.

1985 *Garcia* v. *San Antonio Metropolitan Transit Authority.* Supreme Court rules that Congress can make laws dealing with wages and hour rules applied to city-owned transportation systems.

1989 *Webster* v. *Reproductive Health Services.* Supreme Court holds that a state may prohibit all use of public facilities and publicly employed staff in abortions.

1989 *Johnson* v. *Texas.* Supreme Court rules that flag burning is protected and is a form of "symbolic speech."

1990 *Cruzan* v. *Missouri Department of Health.* Supreme Court recognizes for the first time a very sick person's right to die without being forced to undergo unwanted medical treatment and a person's right to a living will.

1990 *Noriega–CNN* case. Supreme Court upholds lower federal court's decision to allow temporary prior restraint thus limiting the First Amendment right of freedom of the press.

The Birth of the Bill of Rights

"We hold these truths to be self-evident, that all men are created equal, that they are endowed by their Creator with certain unalienable Rights, that among these are Life, Liberty, and the pursuit of Happiness."

THE DECLARATION OF INDEPENDENCE (1776)

A brave Chinese student standing in front of a line of tanks, Eastern Europeans marching against the secret police, happy crowds dancing on top of the Berlin Wall—these were recent scenes of people trying to gain their freedom or celebrating it. The scenes and the events that sparked them will live on in history. They also show the lasting gift that is our Bill of Rights. The freedoms guaranteed by the Bill of Rights have guided and inspired millions of people all over the world in their struggle for freedom.

The Colonies Gain Their Freedom

Like many countries today, the United States fought to gain freedom and democracy for itself. The American colonies had a revolution from 1775 to 1783 to free themselves from British rule.

The colonists fought to free themselves because they believed that the British had violated, or gone against, their rights. The colonists held what some considered the extreme idea that all

James Madison is known as both the "Father of the Constitution" and the "Father of the Bill of Rights." In 1789 he proposed to Congress the amendments that became the Bill of Rights. Madison served two terms as president of the United States from 1809 to 1817.

The Raising of the Liberty Pole by John McRae. In 1776, American colonists hoisted liberty poles as symbols of liberty and freedom from British rule. At the top they usually placed a liberty cap. Such caps resembled the caps given to slaves in ancient Rome when they were freed.

persons are born with certain rights. They believed that these rights could not be taken away, even by the government. The importance our nation gave to individual rights can be seen in the Declaration of Independence. The Declaration, written by Thomas Jefferson in 1776, states:

> We hold these truths to be self-evident, that all men are created equal, that they are endowed by their Creator with certain unaliena-ble Rights, that among these are Life, Liberty, and the pursuit of Happiness.

The United States won its independence from Britain in 1783. But with freedom came the difficult job of forming a government. The Americans wanted a government that was strong enough to keep peace and prosperity, but not so strong that it might take away the rights for which the Revolution had been fought. The Articles of Confederation was the country's first written plan of government.

The Articles of Confederation, becoming law in 1781, created a weak national government. The defects in the Articles soon became clear to many Americans. Because the United States did not have a strong national government, its economy suffered. Under the Articles, Congress did not have the power to tax. It had to ask the states for money or borrow it. There was no separate president or court system. Nine of the states had to agree before Congress's bills became law. In 1786 economic problems caused farmers in Massachusetts to revolt. The national government was almost powerless to stop the revolt. It was also unable to build an army or navy strong enough to protect the United States's borders and its ships on the high seas.

The Constitution Is Drawn Up

The nation's problems had to be solved. So, in February 1787, the Continental Congress asked the states to send delegates to a convention to discuss ways of improving the Articles. That May, fifty-five delegates, from every state except Rhode Island, met in Philadelphia. The group included some of the country's most famous leaders: George Washington, hero of the Revolution; Benjamin Franklin, publisher, inventor, and diplomat; and James Madison, a leading critic of the Articles. Madison would soon become the guiding force behind the Constitutional Convention.

After a long, hot summer of debate the delegates finally drew up the document that became the U.S. Constitution. It set up a strong central government. But it also divided power between three branches of the federal government. These three branches were the executive branch (the presidency), the legislative branch (Congress), and the judicial branch (the courts). Each was given one part of the government's power. This division was to make sure that no single branch became so powerful that it could violate the people's rights.

The legislative branch (made up of the House of Representatives and the Senate) would have the power to pass laws, raise taxes and spend money, regulate the national economy, and declare war. The executive branch was given the power to carry out the laws, run foreign affairs, and command the military.

The Signing of the Constitution painted by Thomas Rossiter. The Constitutional Convention met in Philadelphia from May into September 1787. The proposed Constitution contained protection for some individual rights such as protection against *ex post facto* laws and bills of attainder. When the Constitution was ratified by the required number of states in 1788, however, it did not have a bill of rights.

The role of the judicial branch in this plan was less clear. The Constitution said that the judicial branch would have "judicial power." However, it was unclear exactly what this power was. Over the years "judicial power" has come to mean "judicial review." The power of judicial review allows the federal courts to reject laws passed by Congress or the state legislatures that they believe violate the Constitution.

Judicial review helps protect our rights. It allows federal courts to reject laws that violate the Constitution's guarantees of individual rights. Because of this power, James Madison believed that the courts would be an "impenetrable bulwark," an unbreakable wall, against any attempt by government to take away these rights.

The Constitution did more than divide the power of the federal government among the three branches. It also divided power between the states and the federal government. This division of power is known as *federalism*. Federalism means that the federal

government has control over certain areas. These include regulating the national economy and running foreign and military affairs. The states have control over most other areas. For example, they regulate their economies and make most other laws. Once again, the Framers (writers) of the Constitution hoped that the division of powers would keep both the states and the federal government from becoming too strong and possibly violating individual rights.

The new Constitution did *not,* however, contain a bill of rights. Such a bill would list the people's rights and would forbid the government from interfering with them. The only discussion of the topic came late in the convention. At that time, George Mason of Virginia called for a bill of rights. A Connecticut delegate, Roger Sherman, disagreed. He claimed that a bill of rights was not needed. In his view, the Constitution did not take away any of the rights in the bills of rights in the state constitutions. These had been put in place during the Revolution. The other delegates agreed with Roger Sherman. Mason's proposal was voted down by all.

Yet the Constitution was not without guarantees of individual rights. One of these rights was the protection of *habeas corpus.* This is a legal term that refers to the right of someone who has been arrested to be brought into court and formally charged with a crime. Another right forbade *ex post facto* laws. These are laws that outlaw actions that took place before the passage of the laws. Other parts of the Constitution forbade bills of attainder (laws pronouncing a person guilty of a crime without trial), required jury trials, restricted convictions for treason, and guaranteed a republican form of government. That is a government in which political power rests with citizens who vote for elected officials and representatives responsible to the voters. The Constitution also forbade making public officials pass any "religious test." This meant that religious requirements could not be forced on public officials.

The Debate Over the New Constitution

Once it was written, the Constitution had to be ratified, or approved, by nine of the states before it could go into effect. The new

Constitution created much controversy. Heated battles raged in many states over whether or not to approve the document. One of the main arguments used by those who opposed the Constitution (the Anti-Federalists) was that the Constitution made the federal government too strong. They feared that it might violate the rights of the people just as the British government had. Although he had helped write the Constitution, Anti-Federalist George Mason opposed it for this reason. He claimed that he would sooner chop off his right hand than put it to the Constitution as it then stood.

To correct what they viewed as flaws in the Constitution, the Anti-Federalists insisted that it have a bill of rights. The fiery orator of the Revolution, Patrick Henry, another Anti-Federalist, exclaimed, "Liberty, the greatest of all earthly blessings—give us that precious jewel, and you may take every thing else!"

Although he was not an Anti-Federalist, Thomas Jefferson also believed that a bill of rights was needed. He wrote a letter to James Madison, a wavering Federalist, in which he said: "A bill of rights is what the people are entitled to against every government on earth."

Supporters of the Constitution (the Federalists) argued that it did not need a bill of rights. One reason they stated, similar to that given at the Philadelphia convention, was that most state constitutions had a bill of rights. Nothing in the Constitution would limit or abolish these rights. In 1788 James Madison wrote that he thought a bill of rights would provide only weak "parchment barriers" against attempts by government to take away individual rights. He believed that history had shown that a bill of rights was ineffective on "those occasions when its control [was] needed most."

The views of the Anti-Federalists seem to have had more support than did those of the Federalists. The Federalists came to realize that without a bill of rights, the states might not approve the new Constitution. To ensure ratification, the Federalists therefore agreed to support adding a bill of rights to the Constitution.

With this compromise, eleven of the thirteen states ratified the Constitution by July 1788. The new government of the United States was born. The two remaining states, North Carolina and

Rhode Island, in time accepted the new Constitution. North Carolina approved it in November 1789 and Rhode Island in May 1790.

James Madison Calls for a Bill of Rights

On April 30, 1789, George Washington took the oath of office as president. The new government was launched. One of its first jobs was to amend, or change, the Constitution to include a bill of rights. This is what many of the states had called for during the ratification process. Leading this effort in the new Congress was James Madison. He was a strong supporter of individual rights. As a member of the Virginia legislature, he had helped frame the Virginia Declaration of Rights. He had also fought for religious liberty.

Madison, however, had at first opposed including a bill of rights. But his views had changed. He feared that the Constitution would not be ratified by enough states to become law unless the Federalists offered to include a bill of rights. Madison also knew that many people were afraid of the new government. He feared they might oppose its actions or attempt to undo it. He said a bill of rights "will kill the opposition everywhere, and by putting an end to disaffection to [discontent with] the Government itself, enable the administration to venture on measures not otherwise safe."

On June 8, 1789, the thirty-eight-year-old Madison rose to speak in the House of Representatives. He called for several changes to the Constitution that contained the basis of our present Bill of Rights. Despite his powerful words, Madison's speech did not excite his listeners. Most Federalists in Congress opposed a bill of rights. Others believed that the new Constitution should be given more time to operate before Congress considered making any changes. Many Anti-Federalists wanted a new constitutional convention. There, they hoped to greatly limit the powers of the federal government. These Anti-Federalists thought that adding a bill of rights to the Constitution would prevent their movement for a new convention.

Finally, in August, Madison persuaded the House to consider

his amendments. The House accepted most of them. However, instead of being placed in the relevant sections of the Constitution, as Madison had called for, the House voted to add them as separate amendments. This change—listing the amendments together—made the Bill of Rights the distinct document that it is today.

After approval by the House, the amendments went to the Senate. The Senate dropped what Madison considered the most important part of his plan. This was the protection of freedom of the press, freedom of religious belief, and the right to trial by jury from violation by the states. Protection of these rights from violation by state governments would have to wait until after the Fourteenth Amendment was adopted in 1868.

The House and the Senate at last agreed on ten amendments to protect individual rights. What rights were protected? Here is a partial list:

The First Amendment protects freedom of religion, of speech, of the press, of peaceful assembly, and of petition.

The Second Amendment gives to the states the right to keep a militia (a volunteer, reserve military force) and to the people the right to keep and bear arms.

The Third Amendment prevents the government from keeping troops in private homes during wartime.

The Fourth Amendment protects individuals from unreasonable searches and seizures by the government.

The Fifth Amendment states that the government must get an indictment (an official ruling that a crime has been committed) before someone can be tried for a serious crime. This amendment bans "double jeopardy." This means trying a person twice for the same criminal offense. It also protects people from having to testify against themselves in court.

The Fifth Amendment also says that the government cannot take away a person's "life, liberty, or property, without due process of law." This means that the government must follow fair and just procedures if it takes away a person's "life, liberty, or property." Finally, the Fifth Amendment says that if the government takes property from an individual for public use, it must pay that person an adequate sum of money for the property.

The Sixth Amendment requires that all criminal trials be speedy and public, and decided by a fair jury. The amendment also allows people on trial to know what offense they have been charged with. It also allows them to be present when others testify against them, to call witnesses to their defense, and to have the help of a lawyer.

The Seventh Amendment provides for a jury trial in all cases involving amounts over $20.

The Eighth Amendment forbids unreasonably high bail (money paid to free someone from jail before his or her trial), unreasonably large fines, and cruel and unusual punishments.

The Ninth Amendment says that the rights of the people are not limited only to those listed in the Bill of Rights.

Finally, the Tenth Amendment helps to establish federalism by giving to the states and the people any powers not given to the federal government by the Constitution.

After being approved by the House and the Senate, the amendments were sent to the states for adoption in October 1789. By December 1791, three-fourths of the states had approved the ten amendments we now know as the Bill of Rights. The Bill of Rights had become part of the U.S. Constitution.

How Our Court System Works

Many of the events in this book concern court cases involving the Bill of Rights. To help understand how the U.S. court system works, here is a brief description.

The U.S. federal court system has three levels. At the lowest level are the federal district courts. There are ninety-four district courts, each covering a different area of the United States and its territories. Most cases having to do with the Constitution begin in the district courts.

People who lose their cases in the district courts may then appeal to the next level in the court system, the federal courts of appeals. To appeal means to take your case to a higher court in an attempt to change the lower court's decision. Here, those who are making the appeal try to obtain a different judgment. There are thirteen federal courts of appeals in the United States.

People who lose in the federal courts of appeals may then take their case to the U.S. Supreme Court. It is the highest court in the land. The Supreme Court has the final say in a case. You cannot appeal a Supreme Court decision.

The size of the Supreme Court is set by Congress and has changed over the years. Since 1869 the Supreme Court has been made up of nine justices. One is the chief justice of the United States, and eight are associate justices. The justices are named by the president and confirmed by the Senate.

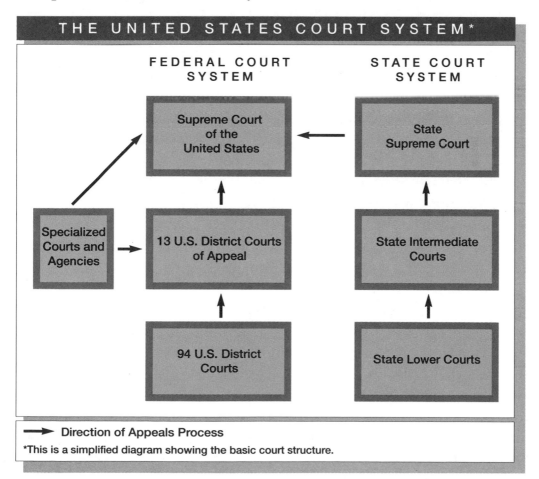

THE UNITED STATES COURT SYSTEM*

FEDERAL COURT SYSTEM

STATE COURT SYSTEM

Supreme Court of the United States

State Supreme Court

Specialized Courts and Agencies

13 U.S. District Courts of Appeal

State Intermediate Courts

94 U.S. District Courts

State Lower Courts

→ Direction of Appeals Process

*This is a simplified diagram showing the basic court structure.

In the Supreme Court, a simple majority of votes is needed to decide a case. If there is a tie, the lower court's decision remains in effect. When the chief justice votes on the majority side, he or she can assign the writing of the opinion to any of the majority justices, including himself or herself. The opinion states the Court's decision and the reasons for it. Who writes the opinion when the chief justice hasn't voted on the majority side? In that case, the longest-serving associate justice who voted for the majority decision can assign the writing to any of the majority justices, including himself or herself.

What if a justice has voted for the majority decision but doesn't agree with the reasons given in the majority opinion? He or she may write what is called a concurring opinion. That is one which agrees with the Court's decision but for different reasons.

Those justices who disagree with the Court's decision may write what is called a dissenting opinion. They have the opportunity to explain why they think the majority Supreme Court decision is wrong.

In addition to the federal court system, each state has its own system of courts. These systems vary from state to state. However, they are usually made up of two or three levels of lower courts and then the state's highest court, usually called the state supreme court. Those who lose their cases in the state supreme court may appeal those decisions to the federal court system, usually to the Supreme Court.

Not all cases that are appealed to the Supreme Court are heard by it. In fact, very few of them are. For the Supreme Court to decide to hear a case, four of the nine justices must vote to hear it. If fewer than four justices vote to hear the case, then the judgment of the lower court remains in effect.

The Ninth Amendment

The Ninth Amendment protects rights of the people, even if those rights are not listed in the Constitution. The amendment was designed to protect the people's rights—but if they are not listed in the Bill of Rights just what are these rights?

From 1791 to 1965, the Supreme Court mentioned the Ninth Amendment only seven times. But in the past three decades, many rights not mentioned in the Constitution have been advocated by various groups. For example, the Supreme Court has used the Ninth Amendment, sometimes in conjunction with other amendments, to declare that there is a right to privacy. This has occurred in Court decisions declaring that laws banning birth control and abortion are unconstitutional. Among the important issues that surround the Ninth Amendment is whether the courts should take an active role in interpreting and even overruling laws and executive actions. Why did the Framers of the Bill of Rights want the Ninth Amendment included? The history of the controversies surrounding this amendment are an exciting part of the history of the Bill of Rights.

The Puzzle of the Ninth Amendment

"The enumeration in the Constitution of certain rights shall not be construed to deny or disparage others retained by the people."

The Ninth Amendment of the Constitution of the United States

In many ways the Ninth Amendment is the most puzzling of the amendments in the Bill of Rights. The Ninth Amendment states, "The enumeration [listing] in the Constitution of certain rights shall not be construed [meant] to deny or disparage [discredit] other rights retained by the people." In everyday language, the Ninth Amendment states that the Framers of the Constitution believed that the rights of the American people go beyond those listed in the Bill of Rights.

But this still leaves a puzzle. Just what are the other rights of American citizens hinted at by the Ninth Amendment? For many years this question went unanswered. During most of our history legal scholars, historians, Supreme Court justices, and others spent their time trying to understand the meaning of the rights already mentioned in the Constitution. For the most part they ignored the Ninth Amendment. In 1955, Supreme Court Justice Robert Jackson

---

The Ninth Amendment states that the listing of rights in the Constitution does not mean to deny other rights to the people—rights that may not be listed. Some people claim that the Ninth Amendment goes even further than covering such unlisted rights as the right to privacy and freedom of association. They say it supports such broad rights as the right to education, employment, housing, income, and medical care.

The Supreme Court has held that the right to vote in federal, state, and local elections is "fundamental," even though that right is not listed in the U.S. Constitution's Bill of Rights.

wrote that "the Ninth Amendment rights which are not to be disturbed by the Federal Government are still a mystery to me."

Over time, the Court began to acknowledge that Americans possessed various unenumerated rights. These are rights not listed specifically in the Constitution. Among the more important unenumerated rights are the right to vote, freedom of association, the right to be considered innocent until proven guilty, the right of access to the political and legal branches of the government, and the right to privacy.

The Supreme Court rarely, if ever, used the Ninth Amendment to justify the existence of these rights. Most of these rights are strongly implied by other parts of the Bill of Rights or the Constitution. For example, the freedom of association is very closely related to the freedom of assembly guaranteed by the First Amendment.

Our nation has undergone many changes since the Bill of Rights was written. American society now is very different from the one in which the Framers of the Bill of Rights lived. Developments in economics, technology, medicine, and other areas have meant new challenges and problems for our nation. Even the wisest and most forward-looking of the Founders of the country could not have imagined the scope of these changes. For example, could George Washington or James Madison have ever imagined television or computers and the ways in which they influence our lives?

Over the past fifty years many people began to believe that these changes have endangered the rights and freedoms of the American people. They argued that the rights set down by James Madison in 1789 could no longer protect our liberties fully. They began to look to the Ninth Amendment as a source for new rights. Since the 1960s, the Ninth Amendment has been used in over 1,200 state and federal court cases. People have claimed that this amendment guarantees everything from a right to privacy to a right to wear long hair or a right to a clean environment.

Various Supreme Court justices have agreed that certain rights are covered by the Ninth Amendment. Since the 1960s different justices have argued that this amendment guarantees the right to privacy, the right to obtain the means of birth control, the right of a woman to have an abortion, the right to marry or not, the right to attend and report criminal trials, among others. Still, a majority of the Court has never declared that the Ninth Amendment offers the only support for the existence of a particular right.

Others have claimed that the Ninth Amendment goes much further, that it supports the existence of many broad rights. Most of these rights relate to social and economic equality. They include the right to education, employment, housing, income, and medical care.

In recent years, the debate over the rights of American citizens has become very important. Some believe that the Supreme Court should exercise judicial activism. This is the belief or policy that as times change the laws should change even though basic principles

Some people claim that medical care is a right. Such a right to medical care is not listed in the Bill of Rights.

don't. According to judicial activism, judges should be free to favor or apply new social policies not always in agreement with previous court decisions. This may mean using the Bill of Rights to expand individual rights beyond just those specifically mentioned in the Constitution. Some cite the Ninth Amendment as evidence and justification for judicial activism.

Others oppose judicial activism. They believe that the Supreme Court has gone too far in expanding individual rights. They argue that the Supreme Court should protect only those rights specifically stated in the Constitution. In their view, the Ninth Amendment is too vague to justify the creation of new rights through judicial activism. Opponents of judicial activism often claim that through such new decisions the Court seems to be getting too involved in lawmaking and executive matters.

This book will first trace the history behind the Ninth Amendment and its adoption. The following chapters will look at how this amendment has been understood and used throughout its history and describe the current controversy surrounding it. The final chapter will discuss the prospects for the expansion of individual rights in the future.

CHAPTER 2

The Birth of the Ninth Amendment

"[A]n omission in the enumeration of the powers of government is neither so dangerous nor important as an omission in the enumeration of the rights of the people."

JAMES WILSON, 1787

When the Founders wrote the Constitution of the United States in 1787, it did not include a bill of rights. The only discussion of this topic came toward the end of the Constitutional Convention. At that time, George Mason of Virginia called for the addition of a bill of rights. Roger Sherman of Connecticut argued against such a bill of rights. He declared that the Constitution did not need a bill of rights, since it did not take away from any state's bill of rights. The other delegates agreed with him, and the motion failed by a unanimous vote.

The new Constitution created much controversy. The debate between the Federalists and the Anti-Federalists focused on two different views of the Constitution. The view of the Anti-Federalists was summed up by one who wrote, "When people institute [set up] government, they of course delegate all rights not expressly reserved." What the Anti-Federalists feared was that the government could do anything that the Constitution did not forbid it

---

James Wilson of Pennsylvania, a leading Federalist at the Constitutional Convention, opposed adding a bill of rights to the Constitution. He said that an incomplete listing of the rights might allow a future government to take away an unlisted right.

35

to do. They wanted a bill of rights that "expressly reserved" the people's rights by stating what the government was forbidden to do. Without this, they believed, the government could violate the rights and liberties of the people.

The Federalists believed that the federal government had only those powers expressly given to it by the Constitution. They claimed that the government could do only what it was allowed to, not just anything it was not forbidden to do. George Washington, who presided over the drafting of the Constitution, wrote, "The people evidently retained [kept] every thing which they did not in express terms give up." Since the people "did not in express terms give up" any of their rights, the government could not violate them.

The Federalists also thought a bill of rights might be dangerous. They knew it was impossible to list all of the people's rights. One Federalist, James Wilson of Pennsylvania, said of this task, "Enumerate [list] all the rights of men! I am sure, sir, that no gentlemen in the late Convention would have attempted such a thing."

Because all rights could not be listed, the Federalists feared that the government might think it could violate any rights that were not listed. Wilson stated that, "in a government consisting [made up] of enumerated powers, such as is proposed for the United States [in the Constitution], a bill of rights would not only be unnecessary, but in my humble judgement, highly imprudent [unwise]." Wilson added:

> If we attempt an enumeration, every thing that is not enumerated is presumed to be given [to the government]. The consequence is, that an imperfect enumeration would throw all implied [unmentioned] power into the scale of the government and the rights of the people would be rendered [made] incomplete. On the other hand, an imperfect enumeration of the powers the government reserves all implied powers to the people; and by that means the constitution becomes incomplete. But of the two, it is much safer to run the risk on the side of the constitution; for an omission in the enumeration of the powers of government is neither so dangerous nor important as

an omission in the enumeration of the rights of the people. . . . To every suggestion concerning a bill of rights, the citizens of the United States may always say, We reserve the right to do what we please.

Wilson gave the example of freedom of the press. He pointed out that there was nothing in the Constitution giving the federal government power over the press. He asked, "What control can proceed from the federal government to shackle [chain] or destroy that sacred palladium [shield] of national freedom?" Wilson said that a bill of rights to protect freedom of the press would be necessary only if "a power similar to that which had been granted for the regulation of commerce had been granted to regulate literary publications."

Alexander Hamilton echoed Wilson's arguments. In the *Federalist Paper #84* he wrote:

Why declare that things shall not be done which there is no power to do? Why for instance, should it be said, that the liberty of the press shall not be restrained, when no power is given by which restrictions may be imposed? . . . [I]t is evident [clear] that it would furnish, to men disposed to usurp [likely to seize power], a plausible pretence [seemingly serious reason] for claiming that power.

Since the Anti-Federalists had much popular support, the Federalists realized that a compromise was needed to assure approval of the Constitution. They agreed to amend, or change, the Constitution by including a bill of rights. This compromise allowed the passage of the Constitution.

James Madison Proposes a Bill of Rights

The task of writing the bill of rights fell to James Madison of Virginia. Though most people in the country supported a bill of rights, few in Congress supported the venture. Many members continued to argue that nothing in the Constitution could be understood as taking away the rights of the people.

Congressman Theodore Sedgwick of Massachusetts argued against an amendment protecting freedom of peaceful assembly. He said that this right was so obvious that no one would ever question it. Sedgwick then told the other members of the House of Representatives that if such an obvious right needed protection, then Congress

> might have declared that a man should have a right to wear his hat if he pleased; that he might get up when he pleased, and to go to bed when he thought proper; but [I] would ask the gentleman whether he thought it necessary to enter these trifles [things of little importance] in a declaration of rights, in a Government where none of them were intended to be infringed [violated].

Despite the opposition he faced, Madison persisted in writing a bill of rights. Madison shared the worry of many Federalists that an incomplete bill of rights might let the government violate any unincluded rights. Madison acknowledged this when he presented his proposed bill of rights to the House of Representatives. Madison stated:

> It has been objected also against a bill of rights, that, by enumerating particular exceptions to the grant of power, it would disparage [harm] those rights which were not placed in that enumeration [list]; and it might be followed by implication [assuming], that those rights which were not singled out, were intended to be assigned into the hands of the General Government, and were consequently insecure. This is one of the most plausible [believable] arguments I have ever heard against the admission of a bill of rights into this system.

Madison did not believe that this meant a bill of rights was unwise. He thought any threat this problem posed "may be guarded against." Madison then cited one of his proposed amendments, which stated:

The exceptions here or elsewhere in the Constitution, made in favor of particular rights, shall not be so construed as [understood] to diminish [lessen] the just importance of other rights retained [kept] by the people, or as to enlarge the powers delegated by the Constitution; but either as actual limitations of such powers, or as inserted merely for greater caution.

James Madison included the Ninth Amendment in what became the Bill of Rights so that the rights actually listed in the other amendments would not be considered a complete list.

This statement formed the basis of what would eventually become the Ninth Amendment. Madison included it to ensure that the Bill of Rights was not considered a complete listing of the people's freedoms. He also hoped it would help protect any rights not listed in the other amendments.

Many ideas and examples influenced Madison's proposed bill of rights. The amendments suggested by the states during the ratification, or approval, of the Constitution were an important influence. Madison's original version of the Ninth Amendment drew heavily on an amendment proposed by the Virginia ratification convention. The Virginia amendment stated:

> That those clauses [statements] which declare that Congress shall not exercise certain powers, be not interpreted, in any manner whatsoever, to extend the powers of Congress; but that they be construed [understood] either as making exceptions to the specified powers where this shall be the case, or otherwise, as inserted merely for greater caution.

Madison's proposed amendments were sent to a committee of the House of Representatives for consideration in July 1789. The committee eventually approved the amendments but changed the wording of some. For the Ninth Amendment, the committee altered the proposed wording to read, "The enumeration in this Constitution of certain rights, shall not be construed to deny or disparage [limit] others retained [kept] by the people."

The full House of Representatives then debated the amendments. The Ninth Amendment met with little opposition. The only discussion came when Representative Elbridge Gerry of Massachusetts suggested changing the word "disparage" to "impair." No other members agreed, and Gerry's suggestion failed to pass. The House then voted to pass the amendment.

After that, the amendments went to the Senate. Since the Senate kept its discussions secret, we know very little of what the senators thought of the amendments. We do know that the Senate slightly altered the wording of the Ninth Amendment to put it in its present form. The amendment now reads: "The enumeration in the Constitution, of certain rights, shall not be construed to deny or disparage others retained by the people."

The proposed bill of rights then went to the states for ratification in 1789. The Ninth Amendment ran into little opposition in most states. In Virginia, though, Edmund Randolph, an important political leader, criticized the amendment.

Randolph believed that the rights in the other amendments "were not all that a free people would require." He thought the Ninth Amendment was too weak to guarantee any other rights. He called it an "opiate," or a drug, that would mislead people into thinking that their unenumerated rights were safe. Randolph and others wanted the Constitution to include stronger protections for individual rights. He also wanted the Ninth Amendment rewritten so that "it could be determined whether any other particular right was retained or not."

Madison opposed Randolph's suggestion. He thought that further restrictions might make the government too weak to run the country. Madison believed that a weak and unstable government was as dangerous to liberty as a government that was too powerful. He wrote to his friend Thomas Jefferson, "[I]t is a melancholy [sad] reflection that liberty should be equally exposed to danger whether the Government have too much or too little power."

While writing the Constitution and the Bill of Rights, Madison had tried to strike a balance between those twin dangers. He wanted a government strong enough to provide law and order, but not so strong that it could easily violate people's rights. He believed that the system he had set up struck a good balance between these extremes.

Madison's arguments won out over Randolph's. Virginia and enough other states eventually adopted the Bill of Rights, including the Ninth Amendment. In December 1791 the Bill of Rights became part of the law of the land and part of the Constitution.

The Ninth Amendment and Unenumerated Rights

"[F]undamental rights, even though not expressly guaranteed, have been recognized by the Court as indispensable to [required for] the enjoyment of rights explicitly defined."

CHIEF JUSTICE WARREN E. BURGER, in
Richmond Newspapers, Inc. v. *Virginia* (1980)

Like some of the other amendments in the Bill of Rights, the Ninth Amendment was of little importance during most of our history. From its adoption in 1791 until 1965, the Supreme Court mentioned the Ninth Amendment in only seven of the hundreds of cases that it decided. Even in these cases, the amendment received only passing notice.

There are several reasons why the Ninth Amendment was so unimportant in this period. During the early years of the United States, the nation focused its attention on forming the government, expanding its territory, and developing the economy. Less attention was paid to protecting personal rights.

Another reason the Ninth Amendment played no important role was that until 1925 the Supreme Court ruled that the Bill of Rights applied only to the federal government, not to the states. In those days, the federal government was very small and rarely did much to

Three of the lawyers who helped win the case against segregated public schools in 1954. In the center is Thurgood Marshall, who later became an associate justice of the Supreme Court. These lawyers worked with the NAACP in the civil rights movement. In the late 1950s and early 1960s, the Supreme Court, in several cases involving the NAACP, upheld the freedom of association.

infringe on people's freedoms. This meant that the Bill of Rights was rarely referred to in federal court cases.

After 1925, the Supreme Court concentrated on establishing and protecting the more specific rights set by the other amendments. Most important cases focused on the rights guaranteed by the First, Fifth, and Fourteenth Amendments. The Court found little need or reason to tackle the vague language of the Ninth Amendment.

This did not mean that the Ninth Amendment was ignored completely. The Ninth Amendment protects unenumerated rights, or rights not listed in the Constitution. In several cases the Supreme Court gave protection to unenumerated rights. In those cases the Court acted in the spirit of the Ninth Amendment, even though it was not mentioned specifically.

The Right to Political Participation

One of the important unenumerated rights is the right to take part in politics, including the right to vote. The Constitution and Bill of Rights do not specifically protect the right of people to take part in the political process. But it is obvious that the Framers wanted the people to have this right. They based the Constitution upon the idea of self-government and active participation by the people in the political process. Voting is the most common form of political participation.

Over time, the Supreme Court came to recognize the unenumerated right of political participation. The first attempt came in 1873. In that year, the Supreme Court wrote an opinion in a case involving a group of New Orleans butchers, known as the *Slaughterhouse* Cases. Justice Samuel Miller wrote:

> It is said to be the right of the citizens of this great country, protected by implied guarantees of its Constitution, "to come to the seat of government to assert any claim he may have upon that government, to transact [do] any business he may have with it, to seek its protection, to share its offices, to engage in administering

its functions. . . ." The right to peaceably assemble and petition for redress of grievances, the privilege of writ of *habeas corpus,* are rights of the citizens guaranteed by the Federal Constitution.

All of these rights mentioned by Justice Miller refer to the right of the people to participate in the political process.

The Supreme Court gave further protection to the right of political participation in 1947. In that year, the Court decided the case of *United Public Workers* v. *Mitchell.* The Court ruled that the Bill of Rights, including the Ninth Amendment, implied a right to political participation.

The roots of this case began in the federal government's response to the economic calamity of the Great Depression. When Franklin D. Roosevelt became president in 1933, he enacted a series of programs that came to be known as the New Deal. The purpose of the New Deal programs was to help fight the Great Depression. One part of the New Deal was to provide government jobs for millions of unemployed Americans.

Many feared that workers employed by New Deal programs would campaign for Roosevelt's re-election. They persuaded Congress to pass the Hatch Act in 1940, which prevented government workers from taking part in political campaigns.

Many government workers objected to this law. They believed they had as much right to political participation as any other citizen. In their view, the Bill of Rights, including the Ninth Amendment, protected this right.

In 1947 the Supreme Court finally ruled on the Hatch Act. The Court agreed that the Ninth Amendment guaranteed the right to political participation. The Court's opinion, written by Justice Stanley Reed, stated:

[T]he nature of political rights reserved to the people by the Ninth and Tenth Amendments [is] involved. The right claimed as inviolate [sacred] may be stated as the right of a citizen to act as a party official or worker to further his own political views. Thus we have a measure of interference by the Hatch Act and Rules with what otherwise would be the freedom of the civil servant [government employee] under the First, Ninth, and Tenth Amendments.

But Reed went on to say that the need to prevent government workers from having too much influence in politics outweighed their right to political participation. The Court therefore ruled that the Hatch Act was constitutional.

In 1958, the Supreme Court extended the right to political participation to include freedom of association. This freedom allows people to form groups, such as political parties or interest groups. Through groups of this kind, people can make their collective voices heard in the political process. Although the First Amendment protects freedom of assembly, the Bill of Rights does not specifically guarantee freedom of association.

The Court's decision came about as a result of a case involving the National Association for the Advancement of Colored People (NAACP) in Alabama. The NAACP is an association devoted to advancing the cause of African-American citizens. During the 1950s, the NAACP took a leading role in fighting for the civil rights of blacks in the South. The state of Alabama had tried with success to prevent the NAACP from operating in the state.

The NAACP took its case to court. It argued that the Bill of Rights and the protection of liberty in the Fourteenth Amendment guaranteed freedom of association, even though the amendments did not mention it specifically. The Supreme Court agreed with the NAACP. Justice John Marshall Harlan wrote, "It is beyond debate that freedom to engage in association for the advancement of beliefs and ideas is an inseparable aspect of the 'liberty' assured by the Due Process Clause of the Fourteenth Amendment."

The Right to an Equal Vote

The most basic form of political participation is voting. Through their votes, citizens can help choose how they shall be governed.

As important as this right is, the Constitution does not guarantee the right to vote. This right, however, is strongly hinted at by the Constitution. The fact that members of the House of Representatives were to be selected by the people shows that the Framers believed in the right to vote.

Because there was no guarantee of the right to vote, many groups have not had this important freedom. For many years women, African Americans, non-landowners, and the young were not considered qualified to vote. This situation changed slowly. By the 1830s, most states had removed the requirement that voters must own property.

The Fifteenth Amendment gave African Americans the right to vote in 1870. Still, many states in the South denied blacks the right to vote. They passed laws requiring voters to pass tests proving their qualifications for voting or to pay a "poll tax" before voting. Since most African Americans had little education or money, these laws prevented them from voting.

This situation continued until 1965. That year, leaders of the civil rights movement persuaded Congress to pass the Voting Rights Act. This act allowed the federal government to enforce the right to vote guaranteed by the Fifteenth Amendment.

Women had to fight for the vote until 1920. That year saw the passage of the Nineteenth Amendment, which guaranteed their right to vote. Finally, in 1971, the Twenty-sixth Amendment gave eighteen-year-olds the right to vote.

The right to vote is usually understood to mean the right to an equal vote. Many would not consider it fair if some people had two or three votes and others only had one. The right to vote would mean much less for those who had fewer votes.

However, an unequal system of voting did exist in many areas of the United States until the 1960s. For example, a district with 1,000 people and another with 10,000 people would each have just one representative in Congress or their state legislature. In such a case, a person in the smaller district had a more powerful vote than a person in the larger district. This meant the right to vote was unequal.

Nothing in the Constitution guarantees an equal vote. In fact, the Constitution set up an unequal voting system for the United States Senate. Each state, whether its population is large or small, has two senators. This means that the Senate representation of people in large-population states is not equal to the representation of people in small-population states.

In 1964, the Supreme Court ruled that the Constitution and the Bill of Rights protected the right to an equal vote. In the case of *Reynolds* v. *Sims,* the Court found that an equal vote was an unenumerated right. Justice William Brennan stated that the right to vote was basic in a free and democratic society. Because of this, the Court would look very closely at any law that limited the right to vote.

Justice Brennan explained that unequal voting systems violated the Constitution:

> Legislators represent people, not trees or acres. Legislators are elected by voters, not farms or cities or economic interests. As long as ours is a representative form of government, the right to elect legislators in a free and unimpaired [unharmed] fashion is a bedrock [foundation] of our political system.

Justice Brennan added that an unequal voting system had the same effects as taking away someone's vote or giving someone a vote that had "two times, or five times, or ten times the weight of votes of citizens in another part of the State." States would therefore have to enforce the rule, "One person, one vote." Since the decision in *Reynolds* v. *Sims* (1964), electoral districts have been divided up so that they contain equal numbers of voters.

Equal Treatment by the Federal Government

Another important unenumerated right is the right to equal treatment by the federal government. There is nothing in the Constitution or the Bill of Rights that says that the federal government cannot discriminate. The Fourteenth Amendment says that the states must provide their citizens with "equal protection of the laws." But this does not apply to the federal government.

Throughout our history many groups have suffered from unequal treatment and discrimination. One of the worst examples has been the treatment of African Americans. Throughout the South, state laws set up a system of segregation, which meant that blacks and whites could not share the same public areas. This forced blacks into separate and often inferior schools, restaurants, hotels, and restrooms.

Discrimination against blacks came largely from state governments, since the Supreme Court failed for many years to enforce the Fourteenth Amendment. The most famous example of this can be seen in the 1896 case of *Plessy* v. *Ferguson*. This case involved Homer Adolph Plessy, an African American who was arrested for riding in a "Whites Only" train car in Louisiana. Plessy and his lawyers argued that forcing African Americans to ride in separate train cars violated the Fourteenth Amendment's protection of equal treatment.

The Supreme Court disagreed with Plessy. It ruled that the Fourteenth Amendment allowed segregation of blacks and whites, as long as both races were separated into equal facilities. Giving the Court's opinion, Justice Henry Billings Brown wrote that segregation did not discriminate because both whites and blacks were affected by the law. He added that if African Americans believed that segregation laws made them feel inferior to whites, it was not the fault of the laws. It was their own fault "solely because the colored race chooses to put that construction [understanding] upon it." Justice Brown concluded by saying, "If one race be inferior to another socially, the Constitution of the United States cannot put them upon the same plane [level]."

Justice Brown's opinion in the case of *Plessy* v. *Ferguson* (1896) reflected the attitudes of the time. Many whites mistakenly believed that African Americans were inferior to them, and they saw nothing wrong with separating the races. The only justice to argue against this view was Justice John Marshall Harlan (grandfather of Justice John Marshall Harlan II). Justice Harlan criticized the Court's opinion as "a compound [mixture] of bad logic, bad history, bad sociology, and bad constitutional law." He added that segregation was wrong because

> in the view of the Constitution, in the eye of the law, there is in this country, no superior, dominant, ruling class of citizens. There is no caste [exclusive group] here. Our constitution is color-blind, and neither knows nor tolerates classes among citizens. In respect of civil rights all citizens are equal before the law. The humblest is the peer [equal] of the most powerful. The law regards man as man, and takes no account of his surroundings or of his color when his civil rights as guaranteed by the supreme law of the land are involved.

It is ironic that this stirring defense of equal rights came from Justice Harlan, a Southerner and a former slave owner.

Not all segregation laws were passed by state governments. African Americans also suffered discrimination by the federal government. Before the 1950s, the federal government had segregated military units, paid black government employees less than whites for the same work, and segregated the public schools in Washington, D.C. (Since the District of Columbia is not a part of any state, the federal government at that time ran its schools.)

After World War II, blacks intensified the fight against the system of segregation and discrimination. One of their first goals was to ban segregated schools. They argued that black schools were inferior to white ones. They believed that this meant blacks were denied "equal protection of the laws."

In 1954, when the Supreme Court decided the case of *Brown* v. *Board of Education of Topeka,* it forbade segregation in public schools. The Court ruled that the equal protection clause of the Fourteenth Amendment prohibited states from segregating schools. From then on, states would have to open all schools to blacks and whites.

On that same day as the *Brown* decision, the Supreme Court also decided the case of *Bolling* v. *Sharpe*. Here the Court struck down the federal government's policy of segregating public schools in Washington, D.C. In doing so, the Court said that there was an unenumerated right of equal treatment by the federal government.

According to Chief Justice Earl Warren, the Fifth Amendment implied a right to equal protection. This amendment states that the federal government cannot take away "life, liberty, or property, without due process of law." The chief justice stated that forcing black children into segregated schools violated their liberty as guaranteed by the Fifth Amendment. From then on, the federal government could not discriminate according to race.

Segregated waiting rooms, restaurants, trains, hotels, and other public places were not considered unconstitutional in the first part of the twentieth century. The Supreme Court had ruled in *Plessy* v. *Ferguson* (1896) that such segregation was allowed if it was "separate but equal."

The Right of the Press to Report Criminal Trials

Another unenumerated right is the right of the press to cover criminal trials. The First Amendment protects freedom of the press, and the Sixth Amendment guarantees public trials for people accused of crimes. But nothing in the Constitution specifically allows the news media to cover criminal trials.

Most trials are open for the news media to report. Sometimes, though, judges have prohibited journalists from reporting trials by issuing "gag orders." Such orders are usually issued in trials where reporting may affect the ability to hold a fair trial.

One example of this took place in Virginia, where a man named Stevenson was tried three times for murder. The third trial ended in a mistrial. A mistrial is declared when the judge rules that the proper procedures have been violated and therefore orders a new trial. Here, a mistrial was declared because the jury had found out about the previous trials from a newspaper. To keep this from happening again, the judge of the fourth trial banned the public, including reporters, from the trial.

Neither the prosecution nor the defense opposed this gag order. But a Richmond, Virginia, newspaper went to the Supreme Court to have the judge's ban overturned. The newspaper claimed that press coverage of trials was an unenumerated right protected by the Ninth Amendment. The state of Virginia argued that the Bill of Rights did not specifically mention any right of the press to cover trials.

This case of *Richmond Newspapers, Inc.* v. *Virginia* was decided by the Supreme Court in 1980. The Court agreed that the Ninth Amendment protected the right of newspapers to cover trials. Chief Justice Warren E. Burger wrote the Court's opinion. He pointed out that the Constitution protects certain rights, even if it does not mention them. In his view, this was why the Framers included the Ninth Amendment. He wrote:

> [T]he Court has acknowledged that certain unarticulated [unstated] rights are implicit [understood to exist] in enumerated guarantees.

For example, the rights of association and privacy, the right to be presumed innocent, and the right to be judged by a standard of proof beyond a reasonable doubt in a criminal trial, as well as the right to travel, appear nowhere in the Constitution or Bill of Rights. Yet these important but unarticulated rights have nonetheless been found to share constitutional protection in common with explicit guarantees. . . . [F]undamental rights, even though not expressly guaranteed, have been recognized by the Court as indispensable to the enjoyment of rights explicitly defined.

Justice William Rehnquist argued against the opinion of the Court. He claimed that the Supreme Court had no right to second-guess a judge who closed a trial to the press. Justice Rehnquist wrote, "I most certainly do not believe that the Ninth Amendment confers upon [gives] us any such power to review orders of state trial judges closing trials in such situations."

The unenumerated rights of political participation and equal treatment and the right to cover trials are closely tied to existing rights and liberties in the Constitution and the Bill of Rights. The Constitution is based upon the idea of self-government, and political participation is very important to self-government. The First Amendment implies the right to take part in politics as well as the right of the press to cover trials. The Fifth Amendment's due-process guarantee suggests that the federal government cannot discriminate against certain people or groups.

By stating the existence of these rights, the Supreme Court seems to have only been filling out those rights already in the Constitution and the Bill of Rights. To do this, the Supreme Court found little need to examine the unenumerated rights protected by the Ninth Amendment. In only a few of these cases did the Court even mention the Ninth Amendment.

But does the Ninth Amendment protect any rights that are not so closely tied to rights already in the Constitution? Beginning in the 1960s, the Supreme Court began to answer "yes" to this question. In doing so, the Supreme Court gave new life to the Ninth Amendment and set off a debate that is still going on today.

The Development of the Right to Privacy

"The makers of our Constitution undertook to secure conditions favorable to the pursuit of happiness. . . . They sought to protect Americans in their beliefs, their thoughts, their emotions and their sensations. They conferred, as against the Government, the right to be let alone—the most comprehensive of rights and the right most valued by civilized men."

JUSTICE LOUIS D. BRANDEIS, in
Olmstead v. *United States* (1928)

"I like my privacy as well as the next one, but I am nevertheless compelled [forced] to admit that government has a right to invade it unless prohibited by some specific constitutional provision."

JUSTICE HUGO L. BLACK, in
Griswold v. *Connecticut* (1965)

The 1950s and 1960s saw a great increase in judicial activism by the Supreme Court. This activism began when Earl Warren became chief justice of the Supreme Court in 1953. Warren helped to steer the Court in the direction of expanding the protection of our constitutional rights. This development is often called the "Rights Revolution." Examples of the "Rights Revolution" include greater tolerance for unpopular forms of speech, increased equality for women and minorities, and increased rights for criminals.

Before 1965, most of the advances in the "Rights Revolution" involved rights enumerated in the Constitution. The Court rarely

---

Dr. C. Lee Buxton and Mrs. Estelle T. Griswold hold Planned Parenthood awards. They had been at the center of the landmark case *Griswold* v. *Connecticut* (1965). The Supreme Court for the first time declared the existence of an unenumerated right not closely related to the others in the Bill of Rights—the right to privacy.

used the Ninth Amendment to protect the unenumerated rights of American citizens. The Supreme Court refused to travel far past the landmarks established by the other amendments in the Bill of Rights. But this began to change as the Court ventured into the uncharted waters of the Ninth Amendment.

The change came with the 1965 case of *Griswold* v. *Connecticut*. This case was important for two reasons. For one thing, it was the first time the Supreme Court declared the existence of an unenumerated right that was not closely related to the others in the Bill of Rights: the right to privacy. In part, the Court based its decision upon the Ninth Amendment's guarantee of unenumerated rights.

The second reason for the importance of the *Griswold* case is that the Court used the right to privacy to strike down a state law that banned the use of birth control. Eight years later, the Court ruled that the right to privacy allowed women to end their pregnancies by abortion. Birth control and abortion are extremely controversial issues in the United States. So with these decisions, the Court set off a heated public debate that has continued to this day.

The idea of a right to privacy involves the claim that the government has no right to interfere in certain areas of people's lives. Justice Louis D. Brandeis described this idea in 1928 when he wrote:

> The makers of our Constitution undertook to secure conditions favorable to the pursuit of happiness. They recognized the significance of man's spiritual nature, of his feelings and of his intellect. They knew that only a part of his pain, pleasure and satisfaction of life are to be found in material things. They sought [tried] to protect Americans in their beliefs, their thoughts, their emotions and their sensations. They conferred, as against the Government, the right to be let alone—the most comprehensive of rights and the right most valued by civilized men.

The idea of a right to privacy existed long before the *Griswold* case. It has its roots in the Bill of Rights. The Third Amendment's ban on the quartering of troops in private homes and the Fourth Amendment's guarantee against unreasonable searches and seizures show the importance the Framers gave to protecting people from government interference in their private lives.

Several state constitutions protect their citizens' right to privacy. The California Constitution says, "All people are by nature free and independent and have an inalienable [undeniable] right to... pursuing and obtaining... privacy." Alaska's constitution reads, "The right of the people to privacy is recognized and shall not be infringed [violated]."

The Supreme Court had begun to acknowledge the right to privacy in the 1920s. In 1923, it ruled that a Nebraska law against teaching German in public schools was unconstitutional. Nebraska had passed this law during World War I, when many people were afraid of anything associated with Germany, including its language.

In the Nebraska case, Justice James C. McReynolds wrote that the Constitution protected certain areas of people's private lives from government interference. These areas included

the right of the individual to contract, to engage in any of the common occupations of life, to acquire useful knowledge, to marry, to establish a home and bring up children, to worship God according to the dictates [rules] of his own conscience, and generally to enjoy those privileges long recognized at common law as essential to the orderly pursuit of happiness by free men.

Justice McReynolds then declared that the state of Nebraska had no right to interfere with the right of parents to educate their children as they wished.

The Supreme Court reaffirmed this principle two years later in the case of *Pierce* v. *Society of Sisters*. This 1925 case involved an Oregon law that required children to attend public schools. Again, the Court ruled that the law interfered with the private area of parents' choices about educating their children.

Extending the Right to Privacy

In 1942, the Supreme Court began to extend the right to privacy into the area of procreation (having children). Earlier, the Court had ruled that states could require "unfit" persons, such as criminals, the mentally retarded, or the physically disabled, to be sterilized (made unable to have children) against their will. In the 1927 case of *Buck* v. *Bell,* Justice Oliver Wendell Holmes had ruled as constitutional a Virginia law that forced mentally impaired persons to be sterilized. "Three generations of imbeciles are enough," he declared.

Justice Holmes's statement seems shocking to us now. But in the 1920s, many people believed that society would be better off if it sterilized various types of people that it considered "unfit." This idea, known as eugenics, called for the sterilization of such broad groups as the homeless, the deaf, orphans, and juvenile delinquents. Eugenics was taken to its most horrifying extreme by Nazi Germany during World War II. The Nazis used their ideas of "racial purity" to justify the murder of people they considered "inferior," including over 6 million Jews who were massacred in Hitler's concentration camps.

In the 1942 case of *Skinner* v. *Oklahoma,* the Supreme Court began to reverse its position. The Court placed limits on the ability of states to require sterilization for certain people. Chief Justice Harlan Fiske Stone declared that these restrictions were necessary because the case involved "one of the basic civil rights of man. Marriage and procreation are fundamental to the very existence and survival of the race."

In 1965, the Supreme Court finally declared, in *Griswold* v. *Connecticut,* that the Constitution protected the right to privacy regarding decisions about having children. The case involved a century-old Connecticut law that made it illegal to use contraceptives (birth-control devices) or to give information about their use. No other state had a law similar to that of Connecticut. Even in Connecticut, this law was rarely enforced.

Then in 1961, Estelle Griswold, the head of Connecticut's Planned Parenthood League (a national organization devoted to family planning) and Dr. Charles Lee Buxton, a doctor at Yale University Medical School, opened a clinic in New Haven, Connecticut. There they provided pregnant women with birth-control information and contraceptives. Soon after opening their clinic, Griswold and Buxton were arrested for giving birth-control information and instructions to a married couple. The two were tried and convicted by a Connecticut state court.

Griswold and Buxton took their case to the Supreme Court. At first their lawyer, Fowler Harper, did not want to argue that Connecticut's law violated the right to privacy. He believed that this argument was shaky, at best. He therefore suggested that they claim the law violated a doctor's First Amendment right to free speech. He thought that a doctor should have the right to give birth-control information to his or her patients.

Eventually Harper found an article in a law journal that claimed that the right to privacy was one of the unenumerated rights protected by the Ninth Amendment. He decided to argue before the Supreme Court that Connecticut's law was unconstitutional because it violated the right to privacy, guaranteed in part by the Ninth Amendment.

The Supreme Court agreed that the Connecticut law was unconstitutional. The seven justices who voted against the law had various reasons for doing so. Justices John Marshall Harlan II and Byron White stated that the Connecticut law violated the Fourteenth Amendment's protection of liberty from state interference. Neither one of them claimed that the Constitution guaranteed a right to privacy.

Five other justices declared not only that the law was unconstitutional, but that the Constitution guaranteed a right to privacy. Justice William O. Douglas, with Justice Tom Clark, declared that the Connecticut law violated "a right of privacy older than the Bill of Rights." Justice Douglas claimed that the right to privacy existed in the "penumbras," or dimly lit surrounding areas of

Justice William O. Douglas served on the Supreme Court from 1939 to 1975. He wrote the majority opinion in the landmark case of *Griswold* v. *Connecticut* (1965). The Court struck down a state law that had made it a crime for even married people to use birth-control devices or to give information or instruction on the use of birth-control devices. The Court ruling extended the right to privacy.

various amendments in the Bill of Rights. These penumbras, according to Douglas, help to give the amendments "life and substance." He argued that the First, Third, Fourth, Fifth, and Ninth Amendments all implied a right to privacy.

Justice Arthur Goldberg, with Chief Justice Earl Warren and Justice William Brennan, took a more direct approach for finding a right to privacy. Goldberg argued that the right to privacy was an unenumerated right protected by the Ninth Amendment. He wrote:

My conclusion that liberty embraces the right of marital privacy, though that right is not mentioned explicitly in the Constitution, is supported both by numerous decisions and by the language and history of the Ninth Amendment, which reveal that the Framers believed that there are additional rights, protected from governmental infringement, which exist alongside those fundamental rights specifically mentioned in the first eight amendments.

. . . [T]o hold that a right so basic and fundamental and so deep-rooted in our society as the right of privacy in marriage may be infringed because that right is not guaranteed in so many words by the first eight amendments is to ignore the Ninth Amendment and to give it no effect whatsoever.

Justices Hugo Black and Potter Stewart disagreed with the rest of the Court. In fact, Stewart believed that the Connecticut law was "uncommonly silly." But both justices strongly rejected the idea that the Constitution guaranteed a right to privacy in the Ninth Amendment or any other area.

Justices Black and Stewart believed that the other justices were engaging in judicial activism by inventing a right that did not exist. They considered this dangerous, since unelected judges were deciding which laws were proper and which were not. Black and Stewart considered this the role of democratically elected legislatures. The only exceptions to this were in the areas specifically protected by the Constitution. Justice Black wrote, "I like my privacy as well as the next one, but I am nevertheless compelled to

Justice Arthur J. Goldberg served on the Supreme Court from 1962 to 1965. In his concurring opinion in *Griswold* v. *Connecticut* (1965), he referred specifically to the Ninth Amendment. He wrote that it "shows a belief of the Constitution's authors that fundamental rights exist that are not expressly enumerated in the first eight [a]mendments." Among these rights was the right of "marital privacy."

admit that government has a right to invade it unless prohibited by some specific constitutional provision.''

After the *Griswold* case, the Supreme Court began to expand the right to privacy into other areas. In 1967, the Court ruled against a Virginia law banning interracial marriages. The Court declared that decisions about marriage were private choices that the government could not interfere with.

In 1972, the Supreme Court extended the right to privacy to include single as well as married people. In the case of *Eisenstadt* v. *Baird,* the Court struck down a Massachusetts law that made it illegal for single persons to obtain birth-control devices. Justice William Brennan wrote:

> If the right of privacy means anything, it is the right of the individual, married or single, to be free from unwarranted governmental intrusion into matters so fundamentally affecting a person as the decision to bear or beget [mother or father] a child.

The *Griswold* and *Eisenstadt* decisions both dealt with birth control and the right to prevent pregnancy without government interference. These decisions by the Supreme Court led many people to wonder whether the right to privacy also included the right to an abortion—the ending of a pregnancy by removing the fetus from the mother's womb.

This was an extremely controversial question. Many people strongly opposed abortion on moral and religious grounds, believing that it was the taking of an innocent life. As the Court began to extend the right to privacy into the area of abortion, it set off one of the most heated political debates of this century.

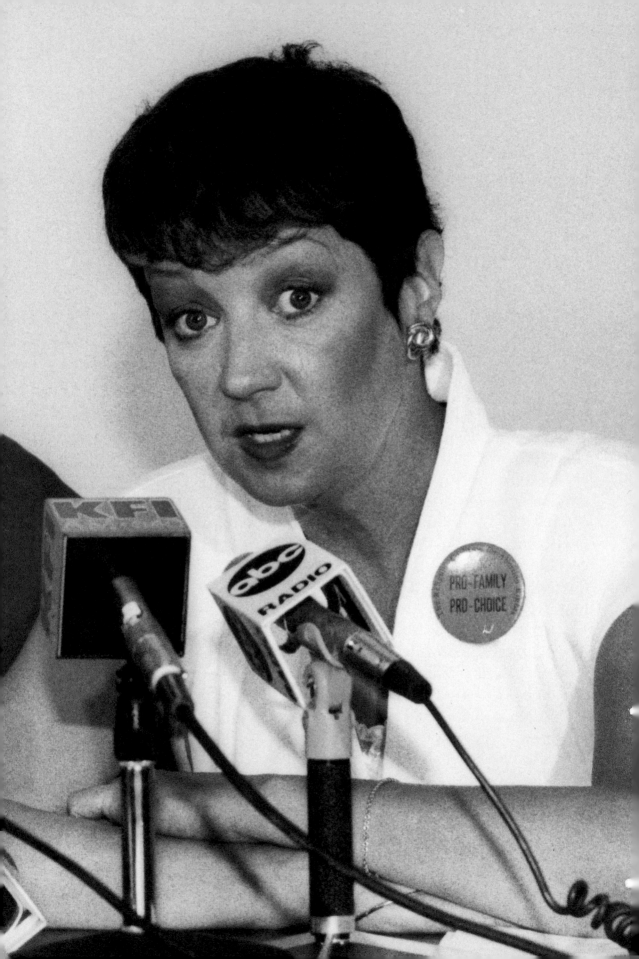

CHAPTER 5

Privacy, Abortion, and *Roe* v. *Wade*

"This right of privacy . . . is broad enough to encompass [include] a
woman's decision whether or not to terminate her pregnancy."

JUSTICE HARRY BLACKMUN, in *Roe* v. *Wade* (1973)

The story of the Supreme Court's first abortion decision began in
Dallas, Texas, in December 1969. Three women met together in a
local restaurant. One of the women, Norma McCorvey, began to
tell her story. She had led a hard life. She had dropped out of the
tenth grade and left home. At sixteen she was married and
pregnant.

When Norma McCorvey told her husband she was pregnant, he
beat her. McCorvey then left her husband and returned home.
Since she was unable to find steady work, Norma McCorvey was
forced to leave her baby daughter with her mother. She found work
with a traveling carnival. When McCorvey returned to Dallas, she
realized that she was pregnant again.

Norma McCorvey was not sure of what to do next. She was
unable to take care of the daughter she had and knew that having
another child would make her already difficult life much worse.
What could she do?

Norma McCorvey, whose case, *Roe* v. *Wade* (1973), resulted in the Supreme
Court ruling that a state law's nearly complete ban on abortions was
unconstitutional. At the time of the case, she was referred to as "Jane Roe."
This photograph was taken at a 1989 news conference.

Ending her pregnancy meant having an abortion, but abortions were illegal in Texas in 1969. Norma McCorvey did not have enough money to travel to another state where abortions were easier to obtain. She could have gotten an illegal abortion in Texas, but she knew that these were very dangerous. Many women had died from unsafe illegal abortions.

Norma McCorvey told her story to Sarah Weddington and Linda Coffee, two Dallas lawyers. They were searching for someone who would help them fight the Texas law against abortions. Such laws, they believed, forced women to make the impossible choice between having children they could not raise or risking their lives with illegal abortions.

Weddington and Coffee believed that they might have a good case with Norma. So they decided to help McCorvey go to court to overturn the Texas law. As they prepared their case, Weddington and Coffee decided to argue that the Texas law violated the right to privacy established by the Supreme Court in the 1965 *Griswold* case.

Both lawyers knew that they faced a difficult task. Most states banned abortions or made them very difficult to get. Many people across the United States were bitterly opposed to abortion. They believed that the unborn child was a person and that abortion was murder.

This has not always been people's attitude. Until the middle 1800s, abortions early in pregnancy were very common. Few people objected, and few states made them illegal.

In those days, most abortions were brought about by having pregnant women take poisons. The hope was that the right amount of poison would abort the fetus, the unborn child, but leave the mother alive. This method did not work very well, however. Many women died from poisoning.

The other method of abortion was by surgically removing the fetus from the pregnant mother. This method was also very unsafe. The surgery was often crude and performed in unsanitary conditions. By some estimates, around a third of all women who underwent surgical abortions died.

Connecticut passed the first anti-abortion law in 1821. Connecticut did this because so many women died during abortions. But the state's lawmakers did not seem motivated by the belief that abortion was wrong. The law prohibited abortion by poison, but only in the latter part of pregnancy. By 1840 only eight states had laws restricting abortions.

The Movement to Outlaw Abortions

The movement to outlaw abortions began in 1857. It was led by Dr. Horatio Storer of the American Medical Association (AMA). Dr. Storer and the AMA believed that abortions were dangerous and should be banned. Eventually, the campaign succeeded in outlawing abortion in the United States.

In the late 1800s, many religious groups had become opposed to abortion. They joined doctors in the campaign to ban abortion. Before 1869, the Roman Catholic church had not taken a very strong position against abortion. But after that, the church declared that abortion was the taking of life. Anyone who had or performed an abortion could be excommunicated, or banned, from the Catholic church.

Many Protestant churches also began to oppose abortion. Knowing that Protestant women had fewer children and more abortions than Catholic women, they worried that the United States would soon be overrun by Catholics. They supported outlawing abortion so that Protestant women would have larger families. At the time, they seemed less concerned that abortion might involve the taking of an innocent life.

By 1900, nearly every state had outlawed abortion. But this did not stop abortions in the United States. Women relied on illegal abortions to end their pregnancies.

Many women died from illegal abortions. This was particularly true for poor women. Wealthy women could usually find a doctor who would perform a relatively safe abortion. Poor women most often had unsafe abortions performed by persons with little or no medical training.

Pro-Abortion and Anti-Abortion Views

Public attitudes about abortions began to change in the 1950s. One reason was that modern medicine had made the abortions performed by doctors much safer. Doctors no longer worried that thousands of women would die if abortions were legalized. They worried more about the dangers that faced women who had illegal abortions.

Another reason for a change in attitude was that the role of women in society was beginning to change. In earlier times, women were seen only as wives, mothers, and homemakers. Now many women began to demand equality with men and more control over their own bodies and lives. They wanted lives and jobs independent of their husbands and families.

Achieving these goals was very difficult for women who became pregnant. So women began to demand more control over when or whether they had children. This led to the increased use of contraceptives and greater demand for legalization of abortion. Eventually, many people came to see the right to abortion as necessary if women were to control their lives. In 1967, the National Organization of Women (NOW) included the "Right of Women to Control Their Reproductive Lives" in their Women's Bill of Rights.

These changes led to many efforts to reform abortion laws in the 1960s. Colorado and California both passed laws making it easier for women to have abortions. But these laws were not very effective. Most women still had to seek illegal abortions.

By 1970, many groups had come out in favor of repealing anti-abortion laws. These included the AMA, NOW, Planned Parenthood, Church Women United, the YWCA, and various religious groups. In the same year, both Hawaii and New York repealed their abortion laws.

The movement to repeal abortion laws led to the mobilization of many people who opposed abortion. These people believed that the fetus was an innocent human life. In their view, aborting a fetus was the same as murder.

The first major anti-abortion campaign was organized in 1971 by Dr. John C. Willke. Willke eventually went on to form the National Right to Life Committee. The Catholic church also began to organize opposition to legalized abortion.

Roe v. *Wade* Goes to Court

The debate over repealing abortion laws was just beginning when Sarah Weddington and Linda Coffee filed their case with the federal court in Dallas on March 3, 1970. Since Norma McCorvey feared the public spotlight, she used the alias, or false name, of "Jane Roe." Her case became known as *Roe* v. *Wade*. Wade was the Dallas district attorney and in charge of enforcing the state's laws. *Roe* v. *Wade* soon became one of the most important cases in the history of the United States.

Roe v. *Wade* was first heard by a panel of three federal judges in Dallas. Both Weddington and Coffee presented the case to the court. They described the Texas abortion law as a violation of the right to privacy guaranteed by the Ninth Amendment. They claimed that the decision to become pregnant or to end a pregnancy was a private choice that the government could not restrict.

Jay Floyd and John Tolle presented the case for the state of Texas. Floyd tried to convince the court that life began at the moment of conception. This meant that the fetus was an unborn person. To abort a fetus, Floyd argued, was murder just as much as killing someone after birth. He claimed that even if a right to privacy existed, it did not allow anyone to commit murder.

Tolle added another argument. He claimed that the decision about abortion should not be made by any court. In his view (similar to the one of Justice Black in the *Griswold* decision), the democratically elected legislatures should decide whether or not a law is proper. The only exception, he said, was where the Constitution stated a specific right, but that was not so with the right to privacy.

On June 17, the judges handed down their opinion. Norma McCorvey had won the first round. The judges agreed that the right to privacy meant that states could not ban abortion. They agreed that "the Texas abortion laws must be declared unconstitutional because they deprive single women and married couples of their right, secured by the Ninth Amendment, to choose whether to have children."

The judges had agreed that the Texas abortion law was unconstitutional, but they refused to order an injunction against the state. An injunction is a legal order prohibiting some action. In this case, it would have kept Texas from enforcing its abortion laws.

Since Texas decided to continue enforcing its abortion law, Weddington and Coffee knew they would have to appeal the decision to the Supreme Court. So they asked McCorvey if she wanted to go ahead. McCorvey was awestruck. She said, "God, the Supreme Court of the United States. My God, all those people are so important. They don't have time to listen to some little old Texas girl who got in trouble." Weddington and Coffee assured her that as a citizen of the United States she had every right to try and appeal her case before the Supreme Court. Norma McCorvey agreed to go ahead.

To the Supreme Court

In December 1971, the Supreme Court heard oral arguments in the *Roe* v. *Wade* case. Since Justices Hugo Black and John Marshall Harlan II had recently died, the Court had only seven members then. Sarah Weddington argued Norma McCorvey's case before the Supreme Court. Again she claimed that the Texas abortion law violated a woman's right to privacy.

Jay Floyd argued the case for Texas. He again claimed that the fetus was a person. Because of this, the state had the right to protect it from death by abortion.

Following the oral arguments, the Supreme Court met to vote on the case. Three justices—William O. Douglas, William Brennan, and Thurgood Marshall—voted to declare that the Constitution guaranteed a right to abortion. Justices Potter Stewart and Harry

Sarah Weddington, a Texas-born lawyer, presented Norma McCorvey's case before the Supreme Court in *Roe* v. *Wade* (1973).

Blackmun wanted to strike down some parts, but not all, of the Texas law. Chief Justice Warren Burger and Justice Byron White believed that the Texas law should be left alone.

The task of writing the Court's opinion was given to Justice Blackmun. Blackmun seemed the obvious choice because of his background in medical law. Before becoming a judge, he had worked as a lawyer for the Mayo Clinic in Minnesota, one of the leading hospitals in the United States. Blackmun knew the importance of the case. He spent many hours studying the issues involved and writing his opinion.

The process dragged on for months. In May 1972, the Supreme Court voted to have the case argued again so that the two new justices, Lewis Powell and William Rehnquist, could become familiar with it. Finally, on January 22, 1973, the Court handed down its opinion in *Roe* v. *Wade.*

The Court voted 7 to 2 that the right to privacy included the right to abortion. Justices Blackmun, Marshall, Douglas, Brennan, Stewart, Powell, and Chief Justice Burger all voted to uphold the right to abortion. Justices White and Rehnquist disagreed with this ruling.

Justice Blackmun wrote that "the Court has recognized that a right of personal privacy, or a guarantee of certain areas or zones of privacy, does exist under the Constitution." He added that the Ninth Amendment was one source of this right. Then Blackmun declared, "This right of privacy . . . is broad enough to encompass [include] a woman's decision whether or not to terminate [end] her pregnancy."

Blackmun went on to say that this right was not absolute. A woman's right to privacy had to be balanced with the states' right to protect the life of an unborn child and the health of the mother. To balance these two rights, Justice Blackmun divided pregnancy into three periods, or trimesters. In the first trimester of pregnancy, he wrote, a woman's right to privacy was absolute. The state could only restrict a woman's right to abortion in this period by requiring that a doctor perform the abortion.

In the second trimester, the woman's right to privacy still outweighed the right of the state to intervene. States could place restrictions on abortions in the second trimester, but only to protect the health of the woman. Only in the third trimester did the state have the right to restrict abortions to protect the life of the unborn child. This allowed states to ban abortions in the third trimester.

Justices White and Rehnquist bitterly denounced Blackmun's opinion. White claimed that the Court's decision meant

> the people and the legislatures of the 50 States are constitutionally disentitled to weigh the relative importance of the continued existence and development of the fetus on the one hand against a spectrum [range] of possible impacts on the mother on the other hand. . . . This issue, for the most part, should be left with the people and to the political processes the people have designed to govern their affairs.

The Supreme Court's decision did not end the controversy over abortion. In fact, it greatly increased the controversy. The issue of abortion was to become one of the most important issues in American politics.

The Right to Abortion Since *Roe* v. *Wade*

"We're talking about an unborn baby who's seeking life. It's a heartbeat, a heartbeat that must be heard and seen."

FLORIDA GOVERNOR ROBERT MARTINEZ, 1989

"[M]illions of women, and their families, have ordered their lives around the right to reproductive choice, and that this right has become vital to the full participation of women in the economic and political walks of American life."

JUSTICE HARRY A. BLACKMUN, in
Webster v. *Reproductive Health Services* (1989)

The Supreme Court's decision in *Roe* v. *Wade* (1973) was met by strong emotions. For those involved in the case there was joy. Norma McCorvey said, "It makes me feel like I'm on top of Mt. Everest."

Most people agreed with the Court's decision. They believed that the Court had done the right thing by affirming the right to privacy and abortion. One poll showed that 64 percent of the public believed abortion should be a matter of personal choice. The leader of one abortion rights organization said, "Reaching farther and deeper and approved by a more decisive vote than we ever expected, this landmark decision established what we have been fighting for long and tirelessly. . . . It was a staggering victory."

But many others attacked the Court's action. Some believed that abortion was wrong and that the government should protect the life of the fetus. The Catholic church was the most outspoken opponent

---

David H. Souter, at his 1990 Senate confirmation hearings. Souter became the first justice appointed to the Supreme Court by President George Bush.

of abortion. John Cardinal Krol, president of the National Catholic Conference, claimed that the decision would lead to the "greatest slaughter of innocent life in the history of mankind." Some Catholics even called for the excommunication of Justice William Brennan, the Court's only Catholic member, for voting to legalize abortion.

Others believed that the Supreme Court had no business declaring abortion laws unconstitutional. John Hart Ely, a famous constitutional law scholar, agreed that abortion should be legalized, but he argued that the issue should be left to the state legislatures. Many others echoed Ely's doubts about the decision.

The Battle over Abortion

Those opposed to abortion immediately prepared to fight. One of their strategies was to restrict abortions through legislation. Senators James Buckley and Jesse Helms sponsored a constitutional amendment to ban abortion. Although a Senate subcommittee held hearings on the issue in 1974 and 1975, the measure never gained enough votes to be passed.

The anti-abortion movement was called pro-life, and it did have some success. In 1973, Congress passed a law that prevented the Legal Services Corporation (a government-run agency for giving legal help to the poor) or any foreign aid agencies from spending money related to abortion. Congress also passed a law that allowed any person or hospital to refuse to perform an abortion.

Another strategy of the pro-life side was to turn public opinion against abortion. Pro-life groups published pamphlets they hoped would show that abortion was murder. They also launched a boycott against the CBS television network for running an episode of the television series "Maude" in which the title character decides to have an abortion. Another tactic of the pro-life groups was to stage protests at abortion clinics and to lobby Congress to restrict abortion.

The final pro-life strategy was to defeat elected officials who supported abortion rights. Most of these attempts failed. One example was Congressman Don Edwards of California. Edwards was targeted for defeat when he refused to hold hearings on a constitutional amendment banning abortion. Despite these efforts, Edwards won a large victory.

Pro-life groups then focused on the 1976 presidential election. In the Democratic primary campaign, Jimmy Carter managed to gain pro-life support by opposing public funding of abortions. This support helped Carter to win his party's nomination.

In the 1976 Republican primary campaign, Ronald Reagan, the former governor of California, was a strong opponent of abortion. He wanted a constitutional amendment to ban abortion. This stand gained him the strong support of pro-life groups in his campaign against President Gerald Ford. Ford took a more moderate position, calling for the issue to be decided by the states. Ford managed to win the Republican nomination over Reagan by a narrow margin. But the Republican party put a plank in its election platform that called for "a constitutional amendment to restore the protection of the right to life for unborn children."

The abortion issue was significant in the 1976 presidential election between Ford and Carter. Both candidates needed the votes of Catholics to win. Both Ford and Carter expressed their personal opposition to abortion, but Ford took a stronger position against abortion. Carter eventually won the election, but only by a very small margin.

Other Abortion Cases

The *Roe* v. *Wade* decision did not end the Supreme Court's involvement with abortion. In 1976, the Court decided the case of *Planned Parenthood* v. *Danforth*. This case began when Missouri passed a law restricting abortions. One provision of this law required women who sought abortions to have the consent of their husbands.

The law also said that women under the age of eighteen had to have the consent of their parents. The state of Missouri claimed that such a law was necessary to allow parents control over their children. Opponents of the law believed that many young women would be afraid to tell their parents they were pregnant and would therefore choose to have unsafe illegal abortions.

The Supreme Court ruled that these Missouri requirements were unconstitutional violations of a woman's right to privacy. It agreed that husbands had an important interest in these matters, but judged that the rights of the wife outweighed this. The Court also said that Missouri had to establish procedures so that teenagers who wanted an abortion could get the permission of a judge instead of their parents.

Despite their other defeats, pro-life advocates won a major victory in 1976. That year, Congress passed a bill that prevented Medicaid (a federal government program providing medical care to the poor) from paying for abortions, except when the mother's life was in danger. Before 1976, Medicaid paid for about one-third of all abortions in the United States.

The law was similar to one passed by several states forbidding the use of state funds for abortions. The Hyde Amendment, named for its sponsor, Congressman Henry Hyde, passed both houses of Congress by wide margins. A similar bill had failed to pass Congress two years earlier.

The law also had the support of President Jimmy Carter. In 1976, Carter had courted the support of pro-life voters by opposing government funding of abortion. He showed his support for the Hyde Amendment when he said:

> [T]here are many things in life that are not fair, that wealthy people can afford and poor people can't. But I don't believe that the Federal Government should take action to try to make these opportunities exactly equal, particularly when there is a moral factor involved.

Many people thought that the Hyde Amendment was unfair. They claimed that by cutting off Medicaid funding, the government made the right to abortion meaningful only for those women who could afford it. This reminded them of the famous saying, "The law in its majestic equality forbids the rich as well as the poor to sleep under bridges and to beg in the streets and to steal bread." The idea here is that rights have little meaning if one cannot afford them.

Opponents of federal funding for abortions believed otherwise. According to them, the Hyde Amendment did not deny anyone the right to an abortion. They pointed out that the right to an abortion did not mean the right to a free abortion paid for with the taxpayers' money. In their view, women who do not want to have a child should make sure they do not get pregnant in the first place, rather than insisting that the government pay for an abortion.

The Supreme Court and Funding for Abortions

The issue of Medicaid funding for abortion soon found its way to the Supreme Court. In 1977, the Court decided the case of *Maher* v. *Roe.* Here the Court ruled that states were not required to provide funding for abortion. Justices William Rehnquist, Potter Stewart, Lewis Powell, Byron White, John Paul Stevens, and Chief Justice Warren Burger declared that these laws did not interfere with the right to an abortion. Justice Lewis Powell wrote that a Connecticut restriction on funding abortions

> places no obstacles—absolute or otherwise—in the pregnant woman's path to an abortion. . . . The indigency [poverty] that may make it difficult—and in some cases, perhaps, impossible—for some women to have abortions is neither created or in any way affected by the Connecticut regulation.

Justices William Brennan, Thurgood Marshall, and Harry Blackmun disagreed with this decision. Justice Brennan wrote that

Students protesting abortion. Thousands of people organized against legalized abortions. Many different groups joined in protest, some people claiming that the millions of abortions that have taken place since 1973 were, in reality, millions of killings. A few extremists bombed abortion clinics.

the other justices had shown "a distressing insensitivity to the plight of impoverished pregnant women." Justice Marshall said that to withhold funding for abortions was "in reality intended to impose a moral viewpoint that no State may constitutionally enforce."

In 1980, the Supreme Court ruled that neither the federal government nor the states had any obligation to pay for abortions. Justice Potter Stewart wrote that while the Constitution protects

> against unwarranted governmental interference with freedom of choice in the context of certain personal decisions, it does not confer an entitlement to such funds as may be necessary to realize all the advantages of that freedom.

Stewart added that Congress could not stop a woman from getting an abortion, but it did not have to make sure she could afford one.

Justices Brennan, Marshall, Blackmun, and Stevens disagreed. According to Justice Brennan, the rest of the Court failed to recognize that by denying funding for abortions, the government "can discourage the exercise of fundamental liberties just as effectively as can an outright denial of those rights through criminal and regulatory sanctions."

On the day that the Supreme Court made this decision, a young mother of four in New York asked if Medicaid would still pay for the abortion she had scheduled for that day. She was told that it would, since the Court's decision would not take effect for twenty-five days. When asked how she would have otherwise paid for her abortion, she said:

> My family doesn't have it, so I probably would have used my welfare check and then eaten from house to house. I couldn't have managed. I love the four children I have, but sometimes I don't have enough milk and diapers for them. So I couldn't clothe another baby. I could barely try to feed it and I wouldn't want to see another child suffer.

The Reagan Administration and the Pro-Life Movement

The pro-life movement gained political strength in the late 1970s. In 1978, pro-life groups helped to defeat several senators and congressmen who supported abortion rights. In 1980, the pro-life groups won an even bigger victory when Ronald Reagan, a strong opponent of abortion, became president.

The Reagan administration supported various efforts to restrict abortion. One of these was a constitutional amendment that would let the states decide the abortion question. Now that the Republican party controlled the Senate, the amendment was passed by a Senate committee in 1982. But despite the lobbying of President Ronald Reagan, the amendment failed to win the two-thirds majority necessary to pass a constitutional amendment.

Another effort of the Reagan administration to limit abortions was to prohibit federal money from going to clinics that performed abortions or gave abortion counseling. President Reagan gave strong public support to the pro-life movement and often met with the leaders of pro-life groups.

The Reagan administration also supported an attempt by the city of Akron, Ohio, to restrict abortions. In the *Roe* decision, the Court had allowed some restrictions on second and third trimester abortions. Akron had passed a city law that required that all second and third trimester abortions be performed in a hospital. This law also required a 24-hour waiting period before any abortion and stated that teenagers must obtain the permission of their parents before they have an abortion.

In 1983 the Supreme Court struck down each part of the law in the case of *City of Akron* v. *Akron Center for Reproductive Health*. Justice Powell again reaffirmed that "the right of privacy, grounded in the concept of personal liberty guaranteed by the Constitution, encompasses a woman's right to decide whether to terminate her pregnancy." He claimed that the Akron law violated this right. Powell wrote that the waiting period and the requirement

President Ronald Reagan supported a variety of efforts to restrict abortions during the 1980s. He favored a constitutional amendment that would have let the states decide abortion regulations. President Reagan also appointed many federal judges whose conservative views might be more in favor of limiting abortion rights.

concerning abortions past the first trimester "imposed a heavy, and unnecessary, burden on women's access to a relatively inexpensive, otherwise accessible, and safe abortion procedure."

Three justices opposed the Court's decision. Two were Justices Byron White and William Rehnquist, who had both disagreed with *Roe* v. *Wade*. The other was Justice Sandra Day O'Connor, who had replaced Justice Potter Stewart in 1981.

Many were unsure how Justice O'Connor, the first woman on the Supreme Court, would vote. As a judge, she had been known for her conservative views. But many pro-lifers accused her of supporting abortion as a state legislator in Arizona. O'Connor's opinion in the *Akron* case showed her strong disagreement with the *Roe* v. *Wade* decision.

Abortion became an important issue in the 1984 election. That year, Democratic presidential candidate Walter Mondale selected Geraldine Ferraro to be his vice presidential running mate. This was a historic choice, since Ferraro was the first woman nominated for vice president by a major party.

The choice also created a controversy. Ferraro was a strong abortion rights, or pro-choice, supporter. She was also a Catholic. Since the Catholic church strongly opposed abortion, some Catholic clergy criticized Ferraro. New York's Archbishop John O'Connor questioned whether good Catholics could vote for a pro-choice candidate.

The Changing Supreme Court

Ronald Reagan's landslide re-election in 1984 offered the possibility of another chance to overturn *Roe* v. *Wade*. The addition of Justice O'Connor to the Supreme Court meant that now three members of the Court—O'Connor, White, and Rehnquist—might vote to overturn *Roe*. If President Reagan could appoint two more justices to the Supreme Court, there would probably be the five votes necessary to overturn the Court's *Roe* decision. Since the justices who voted in favor of *Roe* were increasingly elderly and likely to retire, there was a good chance that would happen.

In 1986, Chief Justice Burger retired. President Reagan appointed Justice Rehnquist as the new chief justice and Antonin Scalia to take Rehnquist's place. As a strong conservative, Scalia represented another vote against *Roe*. Now the switch of one vote would reverse the *Roe* decision.

The opportunity to appoint another member of the Supreme Court came the following year. In June 1987, Justice Lewis Powell announced his retirement. President Reagan nominated Robert Bork to take Powell's place.

As a legal scholar, Bork had strongly criticized the *Roe* decision. Because of this, many pro-choice groups strongly opposed his nomination. Bork eventually failed to win enough votes in the Senate to confirm his appointment.

President Reagan then appointed Douglas Ginsberg. Before Ginsberg's position on abortion could be determined, he was forced to withdraw from consideration after he admitted using marijuana as a young man. President Reagan then named Anthony Kennedy to take Powell's seat on the Supreme Court.

At his Senate confirmation hearings, Kennedy refused to give his position on abortion. But he did agree that the Constitution protected the right to privacy. This showed that he might be willing to uphold *Roe* v. *Wade*.

The *Webster* Case

The first abortion case to come before these justices of the Supreme Court was *Webster* v. *Reproductive Health Services* in 1989. This case involved a Missouri law that placed various restrictions on abortion. One prohibited public hospitals and employees from performing an abortion unless it was necessary to save the mother's life. Another was that doctors would have to perform tests after the twentieth week of pregnancy to determine whether the fetus was able to survive outside its mother's womb.

Supporters of both the pro-life and pro-choice positions recognized the importance of this case. In early 1989, the National Abortion Rights Action League (NARAL) began a campaign to mobilize public opinion in support of the pro-choice position. It ran ads in newspapers around the country. It also organized a march of 500,000 people in Washington, D.C., to show its pro-choice views. Pro-life groups also organized a large rally in Washington and attempted to mobilize public opinion against abortion.

On July 3, 1989, the Supreme Court announced its decision in the *Webster* case. The Court voted narrowly to keep the *Roe* decision intact, but it ruled that the Missouri law was constitutional. Three justices—Rehnquist, Kennedy, and White—voted to uphold the Missouri law. Their written opinions attacked the logic of the *Roe* decision, claiming that states had a right to protect the life of the fetus throughout the pregnancy, not just in the third trimester. Because of this, states could pass laws that restricted abortions in the first and second trimesters.

Justice Antonin Scalia went even further than this view. He wrote an opinion claiming that the *Roe* decision should be overturned and the constitutional right to abortion should be taken away.

Four other justices—Blackmun, Brennan, Marshall, and Stevens—voted to keep *Roe* intact and to strike down the Missouri law. They declared the Missouri law an unnecessary violation of a woman's right to privacy. Justice Blackmun said the Court's opinion "casts into darkness the hopes and visions of every woman in this country who had believed that the Constitution guaranteed her the right to exercise some control over her unique ability to bear children."

Justice O'Connor cast the deciding vote. She voted to uphold the Missouri law. O'Connor ruled that the Missouri law did not violate the right to abortion set up by *Roe* v. *Wade*. In her view,

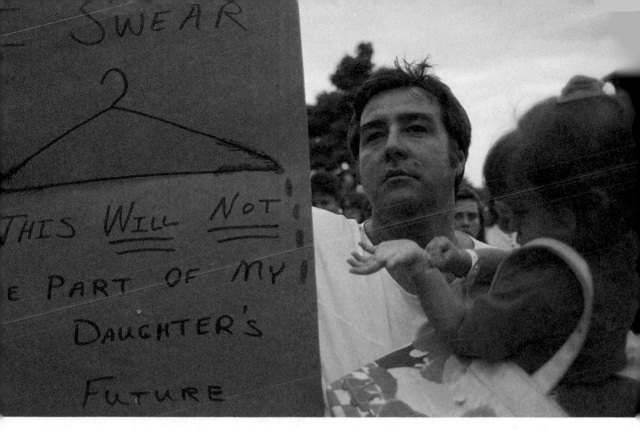

Thousands of people joined in pro-choice rallies across the nation. They protested against limiting abortion rights. Some claimed that a ban on abortions would mean a return to pre-1973 conditions when thousands of women died. They had used dangerous and illegal methods of abortion because much safer methods had not been legal.

consideration of the constitutionality of *Roe* was best put off until some later date.

Though the Court had maintained *Roe* v. *Wade,* it also showed that it would be willing to allow states to place more restrictions on abortion. This decision shifted the abortion battle to the states. Across the country, state legislatures considered passing laws that would ban or limit abortions.

The Abortion Controversy Today

Pro-life and pro-choice groups began large campaigns to influence state legislatures. Both sides mounted petition drives, ad campaigns, lobbying efforts, and public rallies to convince the public, governors, and state legislators to support their side.

The first attempt to place new restrictions on abortion after the *Webster* decision came in Florida. In 1989, Governor Robert Martinez called a special session of the state legislature to pass new restrictions on abortion.

Before the legislature could meet, the Florida Supreme Court ruled that the right to privacy in the Florida Constitution gave women the right to have abortions. Despite this setback, Governor Martinez and pro-life groups were determined to continue. To influence the Florida legislature, they staged a large rally. At the rally, Martinez said that the abortion issue was "about an unborn baby who's seeking life. It's a heartbeat, a heartbeat that must be heard and seen." These efforts, however, failed to persuade the legislature. Within two days, the state senate had rejected all of Martinez's proposals.

Pro-life supporters also managed to have legislatures in Pennsylvania, Idaho, and Louisiana pass laws restricting abortion. The Pennsylvania restrictions were signed into law by Governor Bob Casey. But the Idaho and Louisiana laws were vetoed by the governors of those states—Cecil Andrus and Buddy Roemer.

The politics of abortion played an important role in various elections during 1989 and 1990. In Virginia, Douglas Wilder's support for the pro-choice position helped him to become the nation's first elected black governor. Support for abortion rights also helped James Florio to win the New Jersey governor's race and David Dinkins to become mayor of New York City.

In 1990, the Supreme Court continued to allow states to impose restrictions on the right to abortion. In two cases, the Court ruled that states could require teenagers to notify their parents before they had an abortion. But the Court required the states to provide young women with the alternative of obtaining the permission of a judge.

The abortion question rose again in the summer of 1990, when Justice William Brennan announced his decision to retire from the Supreme Court. Brennan had provided the fifth vote for upholding *Roe* v. *Wade* in the *Webster* case. Supporters as well as opponents of abortion rights sensed that his replacement would determine the future of the issue.

In July 1990, President George Bush nominated David Souter to take Justice Brennan's place on the Court. At his confirmation hearing, many senators tried to discover Souter's beliefs about the right to abortion. But Souter refused to answer these questions, claiming that it would be improper for him to discuss any cases that he might have to decide as a Supreme Court justice. The Senate eventually voted 90 to 9 to approve Souter's nomination, and in October 1990, he joined the other Supreme Court justices. Only when he takes part in deciding a case on this issue, will the nation know his views and the future of abortion in the United States.

The politics of the abortion issue shows the controversy surrounding the Bill of Rights. The issue also shows that the rights guaranteed by that document, including the unenumerated right to privacy, continue to matter in the lives of millions of Americans.

CHAPTER 7

Other Unenumerated Rights

"Education, of course, is not among the rights afforded explicit protection under our Federal Constitution. Nor do we find any basis for saying it is implicitly so protected."

JUSTICE LEWIS F. POWELL, JR., in
San Antonio Independent School District v. *Rodriguez* (1973)

"Only if we closely protect the related interests . . . do we ultimately ensure the integrity of the constitutional guarantee itself."

JUSTICE THURGOOD MARSHALL, in
San Antonio Independent School District v. *Rodriguez* (1973)

The Ninth Amendment guarantees the unenumerated rights that are not listed in the other parts of the Constitution. Over the years, the Supreme Court has given protection to some of these rights: the right to vote, the right of political participation, freedom of association, the right of the press to cover criminal trials, the right to privacy—including the right of a woman to end her pregnancy through abortion—and the right to equal treatment by the federal government. Each of these rights is closely related to and protected by some other amendment in the Bill of Rights besides the Ninth.

This list of unenumerated rights is obviously incomplete. But it is difficult to determine exactly what our other unenumerated rights are. Over the years, people have attempted to find protection for various rights. Usually, they have not succeeded, but these attempts are still important. They show us the directions in which our rights could develop.

A segregated school in 1904. The Supreme Court ruled in 1954 that segregated schools are unconstitutional. But in 1973 it ruled that the Constitution did not guarantee a right to education.

Homosexuals and the Right to Privacy

One direction is to expand the right to privacy. So far, the right to privacy only applies to heterosexual relationships—relationships between two people of different sexes. Many have argued that the right to privacy should also protect homosexual relationships—relationships between two people of the same sex. Supporters of this view argue that the decision to be heterosexual or homosexual is a private decision. Since it is a private decision in their view, they say the government has no right to interfere.

Many people disagree with this position. In their view, homosexuality is immoral or even a sin. They say communities should have the right to pass laws that forbid behavior they believe to be wrong. It is their opinion that the right of the majority to set moral standards outweighs any right to privacy homosexuals might have.

Over the years, support for the view that the right to privacy should include homosexuals has grown. One reason is that the homosexual population in the United States has become more open and outspoken. Another reason is that public attitudes toward homosexuals have become more tolerant.

Because of these changes, many states have repealed their anti-sodomy laws. Sodomy refers to anal or oral sex by homosexual or heterosexual partners, but most sodomy laws are intended to prevent homosexual sex. In 1960, all fifty states had anti-sodomy laws. In 1961, Illinois became the first state to repeal its anti-sodomy law. By 1975, twenty-five other states had followed Illinois's example and repealed similar laws.

Over the years, supporters of homosexual rights have tried to overturn existing anti-sodomy laws. The first important case of this type was the 1975 case of *Doe* v. *Commonwealth's Attorney*. It involved a Virginia law that made sodomy a crime. Those who argued against the law said it deprived homosexuals of their right to privacy. For this reason, they wanted a federal court to declare the law unconstitutional.

Supporters of rights for homosexuals march in the early 1980s. One of their demands was the acceptance of the right to privacy.

The federal court disagreed. It said that the right to privacy guaranteed by the Supreme Court in *Griswold* v. *Connecticut* (1965) only applied to the use of birth control by a married couple. In its view, the right to privacy did not include homosexuals. It ruled that Virginia could pass anti-sodomy laws "in the promotion of morality and decency."

Judge Robert Merhige disagreed with this. Claiming that the right to privacy in *Griswold* v. *Connecticut* protected more than just the right of a married couple to use birth control, Merhige wrote:

[E]very individual has a right to be free from unwarranted governmental intrusion into one's decision on private matters of individual concern. . . . A mature individual's choice of an adult sexual partner, in the privacy of his or her home, would appear to me to be a decision of the utmost private and intimate concern. Private consensual sex acts between adults are matters, absent evidence that they are harmful, in which the state has no legitimate interest.

The next important case involving homosexual rights came in 1984. An officer in the U.S. Navy was dismissed from the military for homosexual conduct. The officer claimed that his right to privacy had been violated.

The federal appeals court disagreed. Judge Robert Bork wrote the court's opinion. Previously, he claimed, the courts had ruled that the right to privacy protected the values of marriage, bearing children, birth control, and family matters. But in Bork's view, none of those values applied to homosexual relationships. He said that the court in the *Doe* v. *Commonwealth's Attorney* case had upheld civilian anti-sodomy laws. Therefore such laws were "certainly sustainable" in the military with its special needs of discipline and good conduct.

The Case of Michael Hardwick

The most important case involving the right to privacy for homosexuals began in 1982. One night Michael Hardwick, a homosexual man, was fined by an Atlanta police officer, K. R. Torick, for drinking in public. Hardwick was confused about the time and date he was supposed to appear in court, and he missed his hearing.

Since Hardwick had missed his hearing, Officer Torick obtained a warrant for his arrest. Michael Hardwick quickly realized that he had missed his court appearance. He went to the court and explained what had happened. The court fined him $150 and gave him a receipt that showed that his arrest warrant was invalid.

Three weeks later, Michael Hardwick was in his bedroom having sex with another man. Hardwick looked up and saw Officer Torick who was there to arrest him for missing his court appearance. The policeman then arrested Hardwick and the other man for violating Georgia's anti-sodomy law.

After Michael Hardwick was released from jail he was contacted by a lawyer from the local American Civil Liberties Union (ACLU). The lawyer talked with him about fighting his case. Hardwick asked what might happen. The lawyer told him that if a judge wanted to make an example of him, he could get up to twenty years in prison.

Michael Hardwick decided to go ahead and fight. Later, he said, "I realized if there was anything I could do, even if it was just laying the foundation to change this horrendous law, that I would feel pretty bad about myself if I just walked away from it."

The local officials in Atlanta knew that Hardwick intended to challenge them. Since they knew they had a weak case, they did not prosecute him. This forced Hardwick to sue the state of Georgia. He claimed that the state's anti-sodomy law violated his right to privacy.

Hardwick's case first went to the federal district court, where Judge Robert Hall refused to hear the case. He said the ruling in *Doe* v. *Commonwealth's Attorney* meant that Hardwick had no case. He wrote, "The Virginia statute [law] challenged in that case is quite similar to the Georgia legislation in question, and all the constitutional arguments made by Hardwick here were rejected in *Doe.*"

Michael Hardwick and his lawyers then appealed his case to the federal court of appeals. Here Hardwick had better luck. The appeals court ruled that Georgia's anti-sodomy law violated Michael's right to privacy. Judge Frank M. Johnson claimed that more recent Supreme Court decisions raised questions about the constitutionality of the decision in *Doe* v. *Commonwealth's Attorney.* Judge Johnson ruled that the right to privacy protected "private consensual sexual behavior among adults."

After Hardwick had won his case, the state of Georgia decided to appeal that decision to the Supreme Court. Before the Supreme Court hears a case, each side and its supporters submit briefs (written summaries of their arguments). Georgia's brief argued that "it is the very act of homosexual sodomy that epitomizes [shows] moral delinquency.'' The brief also claimed that homosexuality leads to a variety of problems. One of these was the spread of acquired immune deficiency syndrome, otherwise known as AIDS.

Various groups filed briefs to support Michael Hardwick's case. The American Public Health Association and the American Psychological Association filed a brief. Their brief noted that studies showed that sodomy was a common practice among heterosexuals. They also pointed out that ''there are great similarities among homosexual and heterosexual couples.'' The brief also claimed that anti-sodomy laws did not help the fight against AIDS and might hurt it by ''driving the disease underground where it is more difficult to study and by impeding the flow of information about prevention from public health experts to the population at risk.''

The Supreme Court heard Michael Hardwick's case on March 31, 1986. Deputy Attorney General Michael Hobbs presented the case for Georgia. He denied that the right to privacy included the right to homosexual sex. Hobbs claimed that if the Court protected this right, it would endanger laws that ban various types of immoral behavior, including adultery, prostitution, and drug abuse.

A justice asked Hobbs why the state of Georgia had not prosecuted Hardwick if his crime was so serious. Hobbs said, ''I do not know what was in the mind of the district attorney when he decided not to prosecute this case.'' Another justice asked whether the law had ever been used against a married couple. Hobbs said that it had not, and to do so would probably be unconstitutional. Hobbs concluded by saying that with this law, Georgia was ''adhering to centuries-old tradition and the conventional morality of its people.''

Michael Hardwick's turn came next. Arguing his case was Laurence Tribe, a professor of law at Harvard University. He said that the right to privacy, guaranteed in part by the Ninth Amendment, should protect homosexuals. Tribe argued that the government should not be able to control ''how every adult, married or unmarried, in every bedroom in Georgia will behave in the closest and most intimate personal association with another adult.''

Michael Hardwick challenged a state law that made certain sexual acts illegal. He won the case in a federal court of appeals that said adults' private sexual behavior was protected by the right to privacy. In 1986, the Supreme Court reversed that decision.

The Supreme Court announced its decision on June 30, 1986. It voted 5 to 4 against Hardwick. The Court's opinion, written by Justice Byron White, said the Constitution did not protect the right of privacy for homosexuals. White claimed that the right of privacy included only matters of "family, marriage, and procreation" that had no relationship to homosexuality.

Chief Justice Burger agreed with the Court's decision in a separate opinion. Burger noted that Georgia's law reflected a long historical tradition. He noted that anti-sodomy laws represented many religious beliefs. In his view, "To hold that the act of homosexual sodomy is somehow protected as a fundamental right would be to cast aside millennia [thousands of years] of moral teaching."

Justice Blackmun wrote an angry opinion disagreeing with the judgment of the Court. He said that "this case is about 'the most comprehensive of rights and the right most valued by civilized men,' namely, 'the right to be let alone.'" Blackmun claimed that the Court's opinion showed intolerance of homosexuals. The fact that there was a long tradition of anti-sodomy laws did not impress Justice Blackmun, who said:

> Like Justice Holmes, I believe that "it is revolting to have no better reason for a rule of law than that so it was laid down in the time of Henry IV [a king of England in the early 1400s]. It is still more revolting if the grounds upon which it was laid down have vanished long since, and the rule persists simply from blind imitation of the past."

Blackmun also disagreed with Chief Justice Burger's statement that religious values supported anti-sodomy laws. He answered it by pointing out that people once used religious teachings to justify the enslavement of African Americans. Blackmun's argument ended with the hope that

> the Court will reconsider its analysis and conclude that depriving individuals of the right to choose for themselves how to conduct their intimate relationships poses a far greater threat to the values most deeply rooted in our Nation's history than tolerance of nonconformity could ever do. Because I think the Court today betrays those values, I dissent.

The Right to Education

Among the other unenumerated rights that people claim, there are certain economic rights. These rights are intended to ensure greater equality between rich and poor. One of them is the right to education. Many people believe that education is necessary if people are to have their other rights and liberties. Without education, the opportunity to enjoy the benefits of life is extremely limited.

People used this argument to protest against segregated schools. Until the 1950s, African Americans were forbidden to attend schools with whites. In the 1896 case of *Plessy* v. *Ferguson,* the Supreme Court ruled that the legal separation of blacks and whites was constitutional as long as the separation was equal. In actual fact, the separate black schools were not equal to white schools. Many people voiced the view that this denied black children the right to education.

In 1954 the Supreme Court agreed. In the case of *Brown* v. *Board of Education of Topeka, Kansas,* the Court ruled that segregated schools were unconstitutional. Chief Justice Earl Warren wrote, "Separate educational facilities are inherently unequal."

Warren claimed that because segregated schools were unequal, black children were denied the benefits of education. According to him, education was necessary for citizenship. He wrote:

Today, education is perhaps the most important function of state and local government. Compulsory school attendance laws and the great expenditures for education both demonstrate [show] our recognition of the importance of education in a democratic society. It is required in the performance of our most basic public responsibilities, even service in the armed forces. It is the very foundation of good citizenship. Today it is a principal instrument in awakening the child to cultural values, in preparing him for later professional training, and in helping him to adjust to his environment. In these days, it is doubtful that any child may reasonably be expected to succeed in life if he is denied the opportunity of an education.

Some people viewed this statement by Chief Justice Warren as recognition that education was a fundamental right guaranteed by the Constitution.

The integration of blacks and whites into the same schools did not end inequality in education. Some schools do not have enough money to provide all that is necessary for a quality education. Many cannot afford good pay for teachers or to buy the computers or audio-visual equipment that good schools need.

This problem is very bad for schools in poor areas. The people who live in these areas cannot afford to support a quality school system. Some people have claimed that students from poor school districts are denied the right to education.

One of these people was Demetrio Rodriguez. Being a father, Rodriguez wanted to make sure that his children received a good education. But Rodriguez worried that this might not be possible. His family lived in a very poor Latino area of San Antonio, Texas. There, people had very little money to support the local schools. Rodriguez's children attended Edgewood Elementary School. This is how Rodriguez described the condition of the school:

> The Edgewood elementary school was an old school, all beat up and falling down. It had a lot of bats, and they [the students] could only use the first floor. Sometimes bricks would fall down. We had a lot of problems in that school, teaching problems and disciplinary problems; they didn't care what the kids were doing.

Demetrio Rodriguez knew that schools in the richer, non-Latino areas of San Antonio were much better. The Edgewood district, where Rodriguez's children went to school, spent $356 on each student. The richer Alamo Heights district spent $594 on each student.

This made Rodriguez angry. He believed his children had a right to a good education, even if they lived in a poor area. So Rodriguez set out to change this. He wanted the state of Texas to make sure that all schools, in rich or in poor areas, had enough money to provide a good education to their students. To do this, Rodriguez took his case to the Supreme Court.

Rodriguez's stand annoyed many people. "They thought I was a Communist," he said. "I told them, I'm no more a Communist than you are. I'm using the judicial system, and I don't care what you say."

Rodriguez's lawyer was Arthur Gochman. Gochman argued that education was a "fundamental right." If something is a fundamental right, then it must be equal for everyone. For example the right of adults to vote is fundamental. This means everyone must have an equal vote. Some people cannot have two votes while other people have only one vote or no vote at all. If education were a fundamental right, then Texas had to make sure that all students had an equal education.

The state of Texas argued against Rodriguez. In the state's view, nothing in the Constitution required it to provide an absolutely equal education for all students. Texas claimed it would be unfair to take money away from the wealthier districts and give it to the poorer districts.

The Supreme Court announced its decision in 1973. In the case of *San Antonio School District* v. *Rodriguez,* the Court agreed with the state of Texas by a vote of 5 to 4. It ruled that the Constitution did not guarantee a right to education. This meant that Texas was not required to provide an equal education for all students.

Justice Lewis Powell wrote the Court's opinion. He denied that education was a fundamental right. Powell wrote: "Education, of course, is not among the rights afforded explicit protection under our Federal Constitution. Nor do we find any basis for saying it is implicitly so protected."

Justice Thurgood Marshall disagreed with the majority opinion of the Court. He wrote that our fundamental rights do not "encompass [include] only established rights which we are bound to recognize from the text of the Constitution itself." He believed that the right to education was important to other rights in the Constitution. So, it needed to be protected if our constitutional rights were to remain secure. Marshall added, "Only if we closely protect the

Demetrio Rodriguez and his wife and daughter. According to *San Antonio School District* v. *Rodriguez* (1973), education is not a fundamental right guaranteed by the U.S. Constitution. But in 1989, the Texas Supreme Court declared that the Texas Constitution guaranteed the right of equal education for all students.

related interests from state discrimination, do we ultimately ensure the integrity of the constitutional guarantee itself.''

    Despite losing in the Supreme Court, Demetrio Rodriguez kept on fighting. According to the Supreme Court, the U.S. Constitution did not guarantee the right to education. But perhaps the state constitution of Texas did. He took his case to the Texas Supreme

Court. In 1989, the Texas Supreme Court agreed with Rodriguez. It declared that the Texas Constitution guaranteed the right of equal education for all students. As a result, it ruled that the state's unequal school financing system violated the Texas Constitution. Several other states have also moved to make sure that students have an equal right to education. The supreme courts of California, Kentucky, and New Jersey have all declared that their constitutions require equal education for all students.

CHAPTER

The Ninth Amendment Today and Tomorrow

"So long as we continue to believe that government is instituted for the sake of securing the rights of the people, and must exercise powers in subordination to those rights, the Ninth Amendment should have the vitality intended for it."

PROFESSOR LEONARD LEVY, 1988

"There is almost no history that would indicate what the ninth amendment was intended to accomplish. But nothing about it suggests that it is a warrant for judges to create constitutional rights not mentioned in the Constitution."

JUDGE ROBERT BORK, 1989

The Ninth Amendment has not been used often. Usually, the Supreme Court has been unwilling to protect unenumerated rights. This is especially true of unenumerated rights that are not closely tied to rights specifically mentioned in the Constitution or the Bill of Rights.

The most famous example of the Court protecting an unenumerated right not closely related to another right was in the case of *Griswold* v. *Connecticut* (1965). In this case, the Court said that the Constitution protected the right of privacy. Even here, only Chief Justice Earl Warren and Justices Arthur Goldberg and William Brennan said that the Ninth Amendment was the sole justification for the right to privacy. Since this decision was handed down, the

As the use of modern electronic equipment grows, many people are concerned about the privacy of their bank records, credit card purchases, and computer communications. Many believe that the right to privacy in such cases is protected by the Fourth Amendment's protection against unreasonable searches and seizures.

Court has become even more reluctant to use the Ninth Amendment.

Despite its rare use by the Supreme Court, the Ninth Amendment is still important. Today, there is a significant debate about the extent of our rights that are protected by the Constitution and the Bill of Rights. In this debate, the Ninth Amendment plays an important role.

Many people, especially conservatives, argue that the Supreme Court has gone too far in protecting rights. They would like the Supreme Court to practice judicial restraint. By judicial restraint they mean that the Supreme Court should not declare laws passed by state legislatures or Congress to be unconstitutional unless they clearly violate a right that is specifically mentioned in the Constitution.

The principle of judicial restraint is the idea that it is more democratic for elected lawmakers than for unelected judges to decide what laws are proper. Many people fear that without judicial restraint our nation will be ruled by unelected judges instead of the elected representatives of the people.

Supporters of judicial restraint oppose the expansion of rights by the Supreme Court. They believe that expansion gives the Court too much power over how our nation is governed. The proper way to expand our rights, they argue, is by amending the Constitution, not by the Supreme Court making up nonexistent rights.

The *Griswold* case offers a good example of the conservative argument. Nowhere does the Bill of Rights mention a right to privacy. Yet the Supreme Court found that the Bill of Rights protected this right anyway. The justices claimed that the right to privacy was implied, or assumed, by the other rights in the document.

Supporters of judicial restraint claim that the Supreme Court should not protect rights, such as the right to privacy, not mentioned in the Constitution. They argue that if the right to privacy is necessary, then the people can pass a constitutional amendment to protect that right. Instead, their argument continues, unelected judges are replacing the Constitution and the will of elected lawmakers with their own views.

But the Bill of Rights is vague. The terms it uses could mean many things. Different people can and do have honest disagreements over exactly what "freedom of speech" or "unreasonable search" or "due process of law" mean. How then should the Supreme Court interpret the Bill of Rights?

It has been argued that the Supreme Court should use "original intent." This means interpreting the Bill of Rights in the way that its Framers intended. To do so, we must look back to what the Framers meant when they wrote, debated, and ratified the Bill of Rights.

For example, does the Eighth Amendment's protection against "cruel and unusual punishments" forbid the death penalty? Followers of original intent would say no. At the time the Bill of Rights was written, the death penalty was common in the United States. If the Framers had intended to abolish the death penalty, they would have said so.

However, it is not always possible to know what the Framers intended. The Framers put few of their thoughts about the Constitution into writing. What documents we do have are often hard to understand, since the meaning of words and ideas have changed greatly over the years. When it is unclear what the Framers intended, followers of original intent propose, the Supreme Court should let elected legislatures decide what the Constitution means.

Other people, especially liberals, argue against judicial restraint and original intent. They believe that it is necessary for the Supreme Court to expand and protect our individual rights. In other words, they want the Court to use "judicial activism." Judicial activism means that the Supreme Court should be willing to overrule laws in order to bring about greater liberty, justice, and equality.

Supporters of judicial activism are less concerned about unelected judges overturning laws passed by elected legislatures. They argue that legislatures reflect the will of the majority. Often, the majority passes laws that unfairly discriminate against the minority. When this happens, the minority has no way to seek change except through the Supreme Court. Supporters of judicial activism point out that this is why we have a Bill of Rights—to protect the rights of individuals from violation by the majority acting through the government.

The example of racial discrimination is used by judicial activists to support their argument. African Americans in the South had no way of changing the laws that discriminated against them. Even if they could have voted, which they could not, they were in the minority and therefore unlikely to elect enough officials who would change the law. Certainly, they could never have gotten enough support to pass a constitutional amendment. The only chance they had of changing racist laws was that the Supreme Court would find those laws unconstitutional.

Judicial activists believe the Supreme Court should not be bound by the intentions of the Framers when determining the Constitution's meaning. One reason is that it is difficult to know exactly what the Framers meant. Another reason is that our nation has changed greatly since 1789. For judicial activists, this means that if the Constitution and the Bill of Rights are to be meaningful today, then they must be understood in a way that reflects the needs of the present, not the past. One example of this is the Fourteenth Amendment (1868). This amendment has provided the basis for many civil rights decisions, including the desegregation of public schools. But when this amendment was first written, segregated schools were common in many parts of the nation, including Washington, D.C. It is obvious that the amendment's Framers did not intend for it to outlaw segregation. In fact, while Congress was debating this amendment, blacks could watch the proceedings only from a segregated area, away from the whites.

Judicial activists argue that if the Supreme Court had followed the original meaning of the Fourteenth Amendment, we might still have segregated schools. Instead, the Court interpreted the amendment in light of the needs of the time. Segregation and discrimination against African Americans had become a national shame. Knowing this, the Court went beyond the Fourteenth Amendment's original meaning and used it to end segregation.

The Ninth Amendment plays an important role in the debate over original intent and judicial activism. Its protection of unenumerated rights is often used as an argument in favor of judicial activism. According to constitutional scholar Leonard Levy:

> Oddly enough, those who advocate a constitutional "jurisprudence of original intention" and assert that the Constitution "said what it meant and meant what it said," are the ones who most vigorously deny content to the Ninth Amendment and to the concept of a "living Constitution."

Levy and others claim that the Ninth Amendment shows that the Framers did not want us to be bound by just the rights they had listed. They believed that this amendment should be used to protect whatever other rights the government might try to take away. In Levy's words:

> So long as we continue to believe that government is instituted for the sake of securing the rights of the people, and must exercise powers in subordination to those rights, the Ninth Amendment should have the vitality intended for it.

Many others reject these claims. If those claims were true, they argue, the Ninth Amendment could be used just as easily to justify the right to sell drugs as the right to privacy. They take the position that we have no way of knowing which rights the Ninth Amendment protects.

The Ninth Amendment and the Bork Nomination

The debate over judicial activism and the meaning of the Ninth Amendment became very important in the summer and fall of

1987. The nomination of Robert Bork to the Supreme Court by President Ronald Reagan in July 1987 led to an important debate over these issues. The Bork nomination forced Congress and the public to consider the best way for the Supreme Court to interpret the Constitution.

The Bork nomination came at a critical time for the Supreme Court. Ever since the late 1960s, conservatives had attempted to undo much of the "Rights Revolution" by appointing conservative justices to the Supreme Court. By 1986, the Court was almost evenly divided between liberals and conservatives. Justices William Brennan, Harry Blackmun, Thurgood Marshall, and John Paul Stevens usually gave a liberal interpretation of the Constitution. Justices Byron White, Sandra Day O'Connor, Antonin Scalia, and Chief Justice William Rehnquist usually took a conservative approach.

In the middle stood Justice Lewis Powell. Powell was often the "swing" vote. He was not solidly on either the liberal or the conservative side. On most issues Powell was conservative. But he often provided the crucial fifth vote for the liberals on such issues as civil rights, the right to privacy, and abortion.

When Justice Powell announced his retirement in June 1987, both liberals and conservatives sensed how important his replacement would be. Conservatives wanted a strong supporter of judicial restraint and original intent. Liberals wanted someone like Powell who might be open to various interpretations of the Constitution.

To the delight of conservatives, President Reagan nominated Robert Bork to take Justice Powell's place. Bork was highly qualified to become a Supreme Court justice. He had been a professor of law at Yale University, solicitor general (the solicitor general argues cases for the United States government before the Supreme Court), and a judge on the United States Court of Appeals.

Bork was also famous for his outspoken, conservative views about the Constitution and the Supreme Court. When President Reagan announced his nomination, he said, "Judge Bork, widely regarded as the most prominent and intellectually powerful advocate of judicial restraint, shares my view that judges' personal preferences and values should not be part of their constitutional interpretations.''

Bork opposed judicial activism and was against unelected judges striking down laws passed by elected legislatures. He wrote:

> What is the good of telling a community that it has every liberty except the liberty to make laws? The liberty to make laws is what constitutes [makes up] a free people. The makers of our Constitution thought so too, for they provided wide powers to representative assemblies and ruled only a few subjects off limits by the Constitution.

Bork also opposed expanding rights beyond those mentioned in the Constitution. For judges to do this, Bork believed, meant falsely assuming that their own values were more important than any others. Bork wrote:

> The choice of ''fundamental values'' by the Court cannot be justified. Where constitutional materials do not clearly specify [show] the value to be preferred, there is no principled way to prefer any claimed human value to any other. The judge must stick close to the text and history, and their fair implications [meanings], and not construct any new rights.

Many liberals feared the appointment of a conservative like Bork. They believed his appointment would lead to the undoing of many Supreme Court decisions that they favored. Most important of these were the right to privacy and abortion, civil rights for minorities, and the rights of people accused of crimes. Senator Edward Kennedy, a leading liberal, strongly criticized the Bork nomination soon after its announcement. Kennedy claimed that if Bork became a Supreme Court justice, ''the doors of the federal courts would be shut on the fingers of millions of citizens for whom the judiciary is—and is often the only—protector of individual rights that are the heart of our democracy.''

Robert Bork speaking at the Senate Judiciary Committee hearings in 1987. Bork favored judicial restraint. He later wrote that nothing in the Ninth Amendment allowed judges "to create constitutional rights not mentioned in the Constitution."

The Constitution states that the president has the power to appoint justices to the Supreme Court, but only with the approval of the Senate. To decide whether the Bork nomination should be approved, the Senate Judiciary Committee held lengthy hearings. The highlight of these hearings came when Bork testified before the committee.

The hearings became a debate over the proper way to interpret the Constitution. Much of this debate centered on the topic of whether the Constitution protected any rights that it did not specifically mention. Several senators believed that the Ninth Amendment justified the expansion of rights beyond just those named in the Constitution.

When Bork was asked about the Ninth Amendment, he compared it to a "water blot" and an "inkblot" that covered over the list of unenumerated rights. In Bork's view, the amendment was useless, since it was impossible to determine exactly what rights might be listed beneath this inkblot. Later, Bork wrote this about the Ninth Amendment:

There is almost no history that would indicate what the ninth amendment was intended to accomplish. But nothing about it suggests that it is a warrant for judges to create constitutional rights not mentioned in the Constitution.

Senator Kennedy argued against this view. He claimed that the Ninth Amendment protected privacy rights,

which are enshrined in such a way and respected and valued so importantly that I would think Americans would have serious questions . . . about placing someone on the Supreme Court that is willing to find some kind of rationale [reason], or appears to find some rationale, not to respect it.

The Senate did not ratify the Bork nomination. Eventually, Anthony Kennedy succeeded Justice Powell on the Supreme Court. At his confirmation hearings, Anthony Kennedy acknowledged that he believed the Constitution protected unenumerated rights, including the right to privacy.

There were many reasons for the Senate's rejection of Robert Bork's appointment to the Supreme Court. One may have been that most people considered Bork's conservative view of rights to be too limited. Most people seemed satisfied that the Supreme Court has interpreted the Constitution and the Bill of Rights to protect certain unenumerated rights from government violation. This seems particularly true of the rights to privacy and abortion.

The battle over how to understand the Bill of Rights continues and is certain to go on in the future. As our nation grows and develops, so will our views and ideas about the meaning of the Bill of Rights.

While this battle continues, the Ninth Amendment is likely to play an important role in it. One of the most controversial aspects of the Bill of Rights is the right to abortion. This right is based on the unenumerated right of privacy, which is protected, in part, by the Ninth Amendment.

The Ninth Amendment will play a leading role as people attempt to claim new rights and liberties to meet the changing needs of our society. These new rights might include the right to privacy for homosexuals or the unrestricted right to abortion for teenagers. Other rights might provide equal education, employment, and medical care for the poor. People who worry about the condition of the homeless argue that there should be a right to adequate housing. It seems likely that they will use the Ninth Amendment to justify constitutional protection of these rights, since they are not mentioned elsewhere in the Bill of Rights.

It seems unlikely that the Ninth Amendment will be used in the near future to expand the protection of unenumerated rights. The present Supreme Court tends to favor judicial restraint when it comes to questions of expanding rights and liberties. The present Court might even limit some rights, particularly the rights to privacy and abortion. Any attempts to expand the protection of unenumerated rights are certain to be controversial. People will argue, groups will march, legislatures will discuss, and the Supreme Court will judge.

IMPORTANT DATES

1787 The Constitutional Convention writes the United States Constitution.

1788 The Constitution is ratified by the states.

1789 The new government set up by the Constitution is put in place.

1789 James Madison proposes the Bill of Rights, and Congress passes it.

1791 The Bill of Rights is approved by the states.

1821 Connecticut passes the nation's first anti-abortion law.

1861 The Civil War begins.

1865 The Civil War ends.

1868 The Fourteenth Amendment is passed. The amendment says that states cannot deny the "privileges or immunities" of its citizens or their "life, liberty, or property, without due process of law."

1870 The Fifteenth Amendment is passed. It gives African Americans the right to vote.

1873 The Supreme Court begins to list the unenumerated rights of citizens in the *Slaughter House* Cases.

1896 In the case of *Plessy* v. *Ferguson,* the Supreme Court says that segregation is constitutional.

1920 The Nineteenth Amendment is passed. It gives women the right to vote.

1923 The Supreme Court first begins to protect the right to privacy in the case of *Meyer* v. *Nebraska.*

1933 Franklin D. Roosevelt becomes president and begins the New Deal.

1940 Congress passes the Hatch Act.

1947 The Supreme Court rules that the Ninth Amendment protects the unenumerated right to political participation in *United Public Workers* v. *Mitchell.*

1954 The Supreme Court declares school segregation unconstitutional in *Brown* v. *Board of Education of Topeka, Kansas.* The Court also implies that there is a right to equal education.

1954 The Supreme Court rules in *Bolling* v. *Sharpe* that the Constitution protects the unenumerated right of equal treatment by the federal government.

1955 The civil rights movement begins with the Montgomery, Alabama, bus boycott.

1958 The Supreme Court strikes down Alabama's demand for NAACP membership lists and declares that the Constitution protects the unenumerated right of freedom of association.

1964 The Supreme Court protects the unenumerated right of an equal vote in *Reynolds* v. *Sims.*

1965 The Voting Rights Act is passed by Congress.

1965 The Supreme Court declares that the Bill of Rights, including the Ninth Amendment, protects the right to privacy in the case of *Griswold* v. *Connecticut.* The Court rules that married couples have the right to use birth control.

1967 The Supreme Court, in the case of *Loving* v. *Virginia,* declares that the right to privacy extends to decisions about whom to marry.

1968 Demetrio Rodriguez begins his fight to have the right to equal education for his children.

1969 Norma McCorvey begins her attempt to have the Texas anti-abortion law declared unconstitutional.

1971 The Twenty-sixth Amendment gives eighteen-year-olds the right to vote.

1972 The Supreme Court, in the case of *Eisenstadt* v. *Baird,* rules that the right to privacy allows unmarried couples to use birth control.

1973 The Supreme Court declares in the case of *Roe* v. *Wade* that the right to privacy protects a woman's right to end her pregnancy by abortion.

1973 The Supreme Court rules that the Constitution does not protect the right to equal education.

1976 Congress passes the Hyde Amendment, forbidding the use of government funds for abortions.

1977 The Supreme Court decides in the case of *Maher* v. *Roe* that the right to abortion does not require state funding of abortion.

1980 The Supreme Court declares in the case of *Harris* v. *McRae* that the right to abortion does not require federal government funding of abortion.

1980 The Supreme Court declares that the Bill of Rights protects the unenumerated right of the press to cover criminal trials in *Richmond Newspapers, Inc.* v. *Virginia.*

1980 Ronald Reagan is elected president.

1981 Justice Sandra Day O'Connor is appointed to the Supreme Court.

1982 Michael Hardwick begins his fight to have the right to privacy protect homosexuals.

1986 The Supreme Court, in the case of *Bowers* v. *Hardwick,* declares that the right to privacy does not include homosexuals.

1986 President Reagan appoints Antonin Scalia to the Supreme Court.

1987 The Bork nomination battle is waged in the Senate.

1987 Anthony Kennedy is appointed to the Supreme Court.

1989 The Supreme Court allows more state restrictions on abortions in the case of *Webster* v. *Reproductive Health Services.*

1989 Abortion becomes an important issue in elections around the country.

1989 The Texas Supreme Court declares that the Texas Constitution guarantees the right to equal education.

1990 The New Jersey Supreme Court declares that the New Jersey Constitution guarantees the right to equal education.

1990 Justice William Brennan resigns from the Supreme Court. President George Bush names David Souter to take Brennan's place. The Senate confirms his nomination.

Glossary

amendment A change in the Constitution.

appeal To refer a case to a higher court to review the decision of a lower court.

brief A written statement prepared for a court in order to support one side in a case. It contains a summary of the facts of the case, the laws involved, and how the facts and laws support one side in the case.

concurring opinion A separate opinion delivered by one or more judges which agrees with the majority opinion's decision but which offers different reasons for reaching that decision.

counsel A lawyer who may appear on behalf of a person in civil or criminal trials or other legal proceedings.

defendant The accused person, who must defend himself or herself against a formal charge. In criminal cases, this means the person officially accused of a crime.

dissenting opinion An opinion by one or more of a court's judges that disagrees with a majority opinion.

executive branch The branch or part of the government that carries the laws into effect and makes sure they are obeyed.

ex post facto laws Laws that make illegal particular actions that took place before the passage of the law.

federalism The relationships between the states and the federal government, each having certain special powers and sharing others.

incorporation The process of making the rights in the Bill of Rights apply to the states so that people are guaranteed to be safeguarded against state actions that might violate their rights.

judicial activism The belief or policy that as times change the laws should change, even though basic principles don't. According to this, judges should therefore be free to favor or apply new social policies not always in agreement with previous court decisions. In some cases, opponents of judicial activism claim that such new decisions are involved in lawmaking and executive matters.

judicial branch The part or branch of government that interprets the laws and settles disputes under the law.

judicial restraint The belief or policy that judges should not apply their own personal views or ideas which may not be consistent with existing laws or court decisions when they are deciding a case. The belief is that courts should not make any changes that could be seen as establishing new law.

jurisdiction The power of a court to decide a legal matter.

legislative branch   The part or branch of the government that makes the laws.

majority opinion   The statement of the opinion of a court in which the majority (more than half of those who vote) of its members join.

original intent   Interpreting the Constitution, including the Bill of Rights, in the way that its Framers intended, or meant, it to be interpreted.

penumbra of rights   The belief that several of the rights guaranteed in the Bill of Rights create zones or areas that extend those clearly named rights. For example, the First Amendment rights of freedom of speech, of the press, and of assembly extend to the right of association. The penumbra (or shadow or zone) of the right of privacy could come from the rights listed in the First, Third, Fourth, and Fifth Amendments and so are implied by the Ninth Amendment.

poll tax   A tax on each person. It was not based on property, job, income, or ability to pay. In the past, the payment of such a tax was sometimes used as a requirement for voting. The Twenty-fourth Amendment (1964) forbade its use as a voting requirement in federal elections. In 1966, the Supreme Court held as unconstitutional its use as a requirement for voting in state elections.

precedent   A previous decision of a court that is used as an example or powerful reason for a same or similar decision in a new case that is similar in facts or principle.

ratification   Approval of an amendment to the Constitution by three-fourths of state legislatures or conventions (after the amendment has been officially proposed by two-thirds of each house of Congress or proposed by a convention called by two-thirds of the states).

separation of powers   The division of the government into three parts or branches—the legislative, the executive, and the judicial.

unenumerated rights   Rights not specifically listed in the Constitution. Among the more important unenumerated rights are the right to vote, freedom of association, the right to be considered innocent until proven guilty, the right of access to the political and legal branches of government, and the right to privacy.

$\mathcal{S}$UGGESTED $\mathcal{R}$EADING

The Bill of Rights and Beyond: A Resource Guide. The Commission on the Bicentennial of the United States Constitution, 1990.

Bork, Robert H. *The Tempting of America: The Political Seduction of the Law.* New York: The Free Press, 1990.

Brant, Irving. *The Bill of Rights: Its Origins and Meaning.* Indianapolis: Bobbs-Merrill, 1965.

*Bronner, Ethan. *Battle for Justice: How the Bork Nomination Shook America.* New York: W.W. Norton, 1989.

Caplan, Russell. "The History and Meaning of the Ninth Amendment." *Virginia Law Review* 69 (1983): p. 223.

Cooper, Charles. "Limited Government and Individual Liberty." *Journal of Law and Politics* 63 (1987): p. 63.

Dunbar, Leslie. "James Madison and the Ninth Amendment." *Virginia Law Review* 42 (1956): p. 627.

*Faux, Marian. *Roe* v. *Wade: The Untold Story of the Landmark Supreme Court Decision That Made Abortion Legal.* New York: Penguin, 1988.

*Irons, Peter. *The Courage of Their Convictions: Sixteen Americans Who Fought Their Way to the Supreme Court.* New York: Penguin Books, 1988, 1990.

Levy, Leonard W. *Original Intent and the Framers' Constitution.* New York: Macmillan, 1988.

Levy, Leonard W., Kenneth L. Karst, and Dennis J. Mahoney. *Encyclopedia of the American Constitution.* New York: Macmillan, 1986.

Massey, Calvin R. "Federalism and Fundamental Rights: The Ninth Amendment." *Hasting Law Journal* 38 (1987): p. 305.

Redlich, Dean. "Are There 'Certain Rights . . . Retained by the People'?" *New York University Law Review* 37 (1962): p. 787.

Rutland, Robert. *The Birth of the Bill of Rights, 1776–1791.* Chapel Hill: University of North Carolina Press, 1955.

Schwartz, Bernard. *The Great Rights of Mankind: A History of the American Bill of Rights.* New York: Oxford University Press, 1977.

*Tribe, Laurence H. *Abortion: The Clash of Absolutes.* New York: W.W. Norton, 1990.

*Woodward, Bob, and Scott Armstrong. *The Brethren: Inside the Supreme Court.* New York: Simon and Schuster, 1980.

*Readers of *The Ninth Amendment* by Philip A. Klinkner will find these books particularly readable.

$\mathscr{S}$OURCES

Abraham, Henry J. *Freedom and the Court: Civil Rights and Liberties in the United States.* 5th ed. New York: Oxford University Press, 1988.

Barnette, Randy. "Reconceiving the Ninth Amendment." *Cornell Law Review* 74 (1988): p. 1.

Berger, Raoul. "The Ninth Amendment." *Cornell Law Review* 66 (1980): p. 1.

Black, Charles L., Jr. *Decision According to Law.* New York: W.W. Norton, 1981.

Black, Charles L., Jr. "On Reading and Using the Ninth Amendment." In *Power and Policy in Quest of the Law,* Myres S. McDougal and W. Michael Reisman, eds. Norwell, Mass.: Kluwer Academic Press (Martinus-Nijhoff Publishers), 1985.

Bork, Robert H. *The Tempting of America: The Political Seduction of the Law.* New York: The Free Press, 1990.

Brant, Irving. *The Bill of Rights: Its Origins and Meaning.* Indianapolis: Bobbs-Merrill, 1965.

Bronner, Ethan. *Battle for Justice: How the Bork Nomination Shook America.* New York: W.W. Norton, 1989.

Caplan, Russell. "The History and Meaning of the Ninth Amendment." *Virginia Law Review* 69 (1983): p. 223.

Cooper, Charles. "Limited Government and Individual Liberty." *Journal of Law and Politics* 4 (1987): p. 63.

Dunbar, Leslie. "James Madison and the Ninth Amendment." *Virginia Law Review* 42 (1956): p. 627.

Ely, John Hart. *Democracy and Distrust: A Theory of Judicial Review.* Cambridge, Mass.: Harvard University Press, 1980.

Faux, Marian. *Roe* v. *Wade: The Untold Story of the Landmark Supreme Court Decision That Made Abortion Legal.* New York: Penguin, 1988.

Gunther, Gerald. *Constitutional Law.* 11th ed. Mineola, N.Y.: Foundation Press, 1985.

Irons, Peter. *The Courage of Their Convictions: Sixteen Americans Who Fought Their Way to the Supreme Court.* New York: Penguin Books, 1988, 1990.

Levy, Leonard W. *Original Intent and the Framers' Constitution.* New York: Macmillan, 1988.

Levy, Leonard W.; Kenneth L. Karst, and Dennis J. Mahoney. *Encyclopedia of the American Constitution.* New York: Macmillan, 1986.

Massey, Calvin R. "Federalism and Fundamental Rights: The Ninth Amendment." *Hasting Law Journal* 38 (1987): p. 305.

Patterson, Bennett. *The Forgotten Ninth Amendment*. Indianapolis: Bobbs-Merrill, 1955.

Redlich, Dean. ''Are There 'Certain Rights . . . Retained by the People'?'' *New York University Law Review* 37 (1962): p. 787.

Rutland, Robert. *The Birth of the Bill of Rights, 1776–1791*. Chapel Hill: University of North Carolina Press, 1955.

Schwartz, Bernard. *The Great Rights of Mankind: A History of the American Bill of Rights*. New York: Oxford University Press, 1977.

Schwartz, Bernard. *Super Chief: Earl Warren and His Supreme Court: A Judicial Biography*. New York: New York University Press, 1983.

Tribe, Laurence H. *Abortion: The Clash of Absolutes*. New York: W.W. Norton, 1990.

Witt, Elder. *The Supreme Court and Individual Rights*. Washington, D.C.: Congressional Quarterly, 1988.

Woodward, Bob, and Scott Armstrong. *The Brethren: Inside the Supreme Court*. New York: Simon and Schuster, 1980.

$\mathcal{I}$NDEX OF $\mathcal{C}$ASES

$\mathscr{I}$ N D E X

Philip A. Klinkner graduated from Lake Forest College in 1985 and is now finishing his Ph.D. in political science at Yale University. He is currently a Governmental Studies Fellow at the Brookings Institution in Washington, D.C. Klinkner is also the author of *The First Amendment* volume in this *American Heritage History of the Bill of Rights*.

Warren E. Burger was Chief Justice of the United States from 1969 to 1986. Since 1985 he has served as chairman of the Commission on the Bicentennial of the United States Constitution. He is also chancellor of the College of William and Mary, Williamsburg, Virginia; chancellor emeritus of the Smithsonian Institution; and a life trustee of the National Geographic Society. Prior to his appointment to the Supreme Court, Chief Justice Burger was Assistant Attorney General of the United States (Civil Division) and judge of the United States Court of Appeals, District of Columbia Circuit.